In Search of Soul

Who am I... Why am I here... What's my purpose?

S'Roya Rose

3RD EYE
PUBLICATIONS

S'Roya Rose Publishing

In Search of SOUL
ISBN 978 0 9923123 8 1
Copyright © by S'Roya Rose, all rights reserved
First Edition Printed 1997
Revised eBook Edition 2008
Revised Printed Edition 2012

All rights reserved. No part of this publication, either in part or in whole, may be reproduced, transmitted or utilised in any form, by any means, digital, electronic, photographic, or mechanical, including photocopying, recording or by any information storage system, without permission in writing from the author, except for brief quotations embodied in literary articles and reviews, credit to be given to S'Roya Rose.

Other Titles by the author:
Reiki a Spiritual Pathway
The Art of Meaningful Living
The Elegance of Being
Awakening the Power of the Goddess
Modern Goddess Oracle Cards
S'Roya Rose Tarot Deck
Blue Moon Oracle Cards

Acknowledgements

My most heartfelt thanks to all the wonderful people whom I have had the pleasure to meet along my life's path. You will never know how it is that you have taught me much about life and especially about myself.

To some very inspirational friends. Without their part in encouraging and consoling me, I may never have began writing this book in the first place.

To all those who I love dearly such as my Mother for her unconditional love and patience, my two daughters, Tamaya and Cortnei, for gracing me with their love and beautiful presence, my many friends, especially Keith and Diacon who were always there for me, I love you all and thank you for being part of my live.

To the man without whom I would never have mastered the computer nor began writing this book, who's unconditional love and encouragement shines a light in my heart that will burn forever. I speak of the first editor of this book, Brian Priest from the Oracle Press. You hold a special place in my heart always. Thank you all for your love, patience and unwavering support.

Many Blessings

S'Roya Rose

S'Roya Rose
www.sroyarose.com
email@sroyarose.com

Contents

1. A Message from Soul... **8**

2. In Search of Soul... **11**

3. Soul verses Ego... **25**

4. Castle of our Mind... **39**

5. Doorways to the Soul... **55**

6. Upon Love the Soul Walks... **67**

7. The Journey Within... **85**

8. Mastery of Self... **94**

A Message from S'Roya

This is a beginners book written to help those seeking some answers to those infamous life questions. Who am I, why am I here, and what's my purpose? Are questions that send us on a quest for truth. Some of what's written may confirm what you already know, some of it will serve to fill in the gaps, while for others it will challenge your current beliefs and hopefully open your mind for you to experience a broader better life.

There are many more attributes to the human experience of learning, which are covered in the following chapters. Life is a circle of self realisation, sooner or later we all get with the program. It will enlighten you as to how your deep inner needs are the wishes of the soul.

This book is designed to take you on a journey through the many attributes of self and show simply how these all come into play in one form or another.

It is meant to validate and enlighten the inner struggles of mankind and help with the evolvement of our consciousness. It is only by raising our conscious awareness that we can begin to live our lives more fully and still be true to self and others.

Our planet is undergoing many changes and we are having to change with this, but if we are all caught up in wars, money worries, power struggles and personality conflicts and the like, how is it ever going to be possible for us to get beyond these struggles? If I have learnt anything it is that everything we push against or resist we actually bring towards us. And so it is that we must start with changing and improving ourselves before we can implement the right changes to make the world a better place for everyone to live.

If every one sought to look after self and take the responsibilities of such, we would not have to lean on others for our existence, support would be the natural order of things. We would be free to support each other and help each other to coexist. Instead of judging who is right and who is wrong, we could all just be! It is this continual battle with egos that keeps countries poor and at war with each other. So preoccupied is man with what is going on in the physical world that he has forgotten why he is here, totally losing the plot.

The purpose of this book is to expose the simple things that makes us human and *how our soul, as subtle as it is, plays a huge part in our lives.*

It explains more fully the soul, what it is, how it works and why we need to connect with it. If we all learned to seek out our soul and its real purpose, instead of more money or more land or power, there would be plenty to do without all the bickering and pettiness.

The other thing we all need to understand is that as men and women we were always equal, but we are also different. It is our differences that we have been sorting out and coming to terms with in the past few centuries.

Now, we should have no more reason to quarrel between the sexes. They both perform their equal functions and for this, deserve mutual respect.

Men have had much to learn about sharing and showing real honest emotion. This does not come natural to them, unlike women who know how to share and show compassion whilst being in touch with our emotions.

The male and female energies on the planet are becoming more integrated, as our duality evolves. This will help to bring more balance into our lives. My hope is that you find this book interesting and cannot put it down. If only one thing in this book helps make a difference to your conscious awareness, then my job as the author is done and I will be happy for you. It is my belief that upon sharing information about the nature of human development, that we will all grow and become better citizens and keepers of this beautiful planet.

We Are

We are not the colour of our hair
nor the colour of our skin.
We are not the country of our birth
where our origin begins.
We are not the lessons that were taught
from teachers in our schools.
We are not the language that we speak
of which our life makes rules.
We are not the food that we eat
nor the water of which we drink.
We are but the quality of our deeds
and of how we feel and think.

Chapter 1
In Search of Soul

As we feel ourselves heading towards our future at an ever increasing pace, with our lives buried under a myriad of circumstance, one wonders what it has all been for; life I mean!? How many of us find ourselves numbed by the continual regularity of a nine-to-five job, paying the mortgage, putting food on the table and a roof over the heads of loved ones? All this while trying to juggle a career with a love life, children's needs, trips to the vet with family pets and the never ending bills. Sound familiar to you? I'm sure it does.

As I reflect back to a time during my twenties, I asked myself that very question. I had done what most people thought were the right things to do in life. I built a career, married young and settled down to raise a family with a man whom I thought would make a good husband.

Six years later I was separated with two young children to support. I was alone, disillusioned, frightened and very unhappy, believing that I was a disappointment to my parents. I saw myself a complete failure at life and my marriage was in tatters. Where did I go wrong? What was the answer?

As we look back over our lives we can see there were many things that influenced it to change, but none more so than the crisis and trauma of a marriage or relationship breakdown. I realised much later that my mistakes lay with the fact I was too young to know myself, never mind anyone else, and that I had made a bad choice for a life partner.

This life change sent me on another learning curve that took many more years to complete. It sent me in search of something that I didn't know existed at that time. This book is dedicated to the search I began many years ago; the search for myself and my soul.

To be truly happy with life and have love and a purpose for being is our real destiny, but as our life gets complicated this idea takes on the feeling of sheer folly. The truth of the matter is that we could feel loved each day and we could do what makes us feel good for a living while feeding our purpose. First we need to stop and ask ourselves some questions. It isn't until we do this that we open up for the true answers. Be prepared though; we need to be taught about all aspects of self and these answers will come in many different ways.

Until we stop and look at oour life and ask ourselves some soul-searching questions, it will never improve. This questioning is a call from the soul asking us to look at our life more closely with the desire to make it work.

It usually doesn't happen until there is some reason or catalyst, such as a life threatening disease, a death or the loss of a loved one, maybe a heart attack, or a breakdown of some sort from sheer exhaustion.

> ### The questions
>
> What is the meaning of life, to love, learn, or play?
> Why am I asking? Why do I have to stay?
> I don't need to be here in this time or place,
> but my wish is to stay and help the human race.
> Life is a continuation of moments, that's all,
> the day we are born we've answered the call.
> Feeling and living each moment is the test,
> of this journey they call our life-long quest.
> Pleasures are experience, not the coming or going,
> it's in the message we find through our inner knowing.
> So seek out your soul and allow yourself to be,
> for in the Afterlife you'll know what you cannot see.

Perhaps you are tired of the sameness in your life and feel empty even with all you have accomplished. Or maybe you find it hard to get work and can't work out why. You may feel there must be more to life and that something is missing in yours.

Some of the biggest catalysts for soul searching has been the breakdown of personal relationships and marriages, the pursuit of real love and the seeking of financial security through career or business. The stress of these takes its toll, along with the pressures of society, beckoning us to have everything to satisfy our ego's ever consuming needs.

For some, even after they have completed all their set goals in life, there is an emptiness that still haunts them and they begin to ask, what is this all for? There must be more meaning to life. This seems to be just one of the things that we are driven to do; an instinct if you like that we all seem to follow. We want to get it right, for one reason or another, at least once in our lives, whether it is work, home environment, love life or our search for inner peace.

We need to know the answers to be able to correct it and get it right. All of these things eventually leads us to the crossroads in our mind that asks, what is this all about and why am I here? Do I have a purpose and what is my reason for being? Until you stop and ask these questions you will not hear the call of your soul.

> Ask and it shall be given to you;
> seek and ye shall find;
> knock and it shall be opened unto you.
> For everyone that asketh, receiveth;
> and he that seeketh, findeth;
> and to him that knocketh it shall be opened.
>
> - HOLY BIBLE

What is soul and why do we need to listen to it or go in search of it? Soul is the very essence of who you are, the core of your individuality. The soul is the creative you, the spontaneous you, the compassionate you, the heart of you. It's the part of you that connects with All That Is, and sees the bigger picture. Soul is the part of your high mindedness that knows and feels a deeper meaning.

It seeks to fulfill you with the highest quality of thoughts and feelings, helping you to live a more meaningful life. It connects you to your spirit giving you courage to be who you truly are.

Dancers, painters, writers and musicians all connect with their soul through their creative talents. We are quite often moved by the things they do as it connects with our soul.

Music can invoke tears, dancing gives us a sense of play and joy, paintings make us think and philosophise, and the written word lets us know we are not alone in our thinking. Soul gives feeling to whatever we think, say or do. It's the point where everything has a principal meaning for us. It's no wonder we go in search of our soul because it puts more meaning back into our life. When we answer the call of our soul we are answering the call to live! Your soul is the totality of who you really are; past, present and future.

> Who I once was
> Who I am now
> Who I could be!

When we go in search of soul we are searching for self, the self we have forgotten about but need to connect with to make sense of it all. For some people this is a discovery of true inner spirit; for others it is conformation of growth and practical mental processes, for most it is a time of enlightenment of self.

For some this call happens early in their life and for others it happens much later. It doesn't matter because whenever it arrives you will know. There will be no turning back until you have all your answers. These answers will help you to make sense out of your life so that you will feel empowered and continue the journey.

Looking back I can remember different times when my mind turned inward so that I could hear my soul speak, helping me understand my circumstances. This was very painful at times, but led to my discovering some truths about what was not working in my life and why I was so unhappy. It allowed me the opportunity, in the form of choices, to do something about this, helping me to take back the responsibility for my life's destiny.

Destiny

> Destiny is a paradox of which I know not,
> the aspirations to go forth from this our lot,
> or a word we choose to explain our lives.
> Is it the motive behind our action that drives?
> Does our super-conscious tell us how to act?
> Are we destined for this or destined for that?
> Is it all planned before this earth we appear?
> Are these the questions of destiny you fear?
> If there are any doubts about your life's call,
> then you're not alone with these thoughts at all.
> For destiny does play along with chance,
> throughout your life full of circumstance.
> The riddles of which you need to unfold,
> to live your life fully is both noble and bold.

We all get inklings of our future destiny through our sleep in dreams, and through the hearts desires for things we feel compelled to do. However, we do not trust these feelings as guidance or messages from soul, or destiny knocking.

I remember how bogged down I became in my own emotional despair. It never occurred to me to think about guidance or intuitive thought or destiny. It wasn't until later when I looked back at some of the messages I had received at those crisis times that I realised how they had helped.

During one of the many deep and meaningful philosophical discussions with a friend, I was asked what I thought my destiny was. I had no idea what he meant and wasn't sure what destiny was. So then I began to ask questions about this and what it meant to others, discovering then why I didn't know.

Moving onto Change

I began to make some decisions about what I didn't want in my life anymore. While trying not to allow any more circumstances to dictate my future I cleared away some of the unwanted debris. This was in many forms; monitory worries, people I wished not to be involved with anymore, places I no longer wanted to go, the jobs and circumstances I no longer wished to be associated with. Some of this debris was in a physical form in my everyday life with things that surrounded me, but some of it was also within my own mind and behaviour.

I wanted desperately to change some of my emotional reactions and negative attitudes. As I look at some of the beliefs I had at the time it is no wonder I felt the way I did.

People had asked me what did I want out of life? I could not in all honesty answer this question with any real clarity. It served to frustrate me as I had no idea what I wanted out of life or what I would do given the chance to choose.

It wasn't until I began to look at those things that I no longer wanted that the path to what I did want slowly became clearer and so I changed them. Knowing what you don't want puts you on the road to what you really desire. Only then could I focus on how I really felt without all the burdens and encumbrances that clouded and hindered my mind and life. As a result of this, I began to understand myself better and could see who I had become as I looked at my life's path more closely.

Discovering my strengths and exposing my weaknesses meant peeling away many layers of beliefs and taking a good hard look at myself. I became aware of how my life had unfolded and how I had reacted to my childhood and schooling, family and peers, boys and love, work and money, marriage and children; physically, emotionally, mentally and spiritually. My dramas and attitudes were exposed and I could see how they had shaped my life.

Now armed, I took up my sword and shield of self discovery with a vengeance, wanting in haste to push away the past layers of outdated beliefs that my life had imposed on me. I was busy finding out what was worthy of me now and what did not belong to the person who I had become.

> *I was a warrior in pursuit of my Soul
> looking for my Holy Grail.
> My inner knowing was now at war
> with the beliefs of my experience about life.*

Have you not heard your soul knocking at the door and the wind chimes of life calling for you to embark on your real pilgrimage? I felt for some time that our hearts are on the freeway but our souls are on the runway, waiting, until we give them flight. Have you not felt that if you had wings to soar high above the mountains and valleys of life, viewing it from above, that you would know what it is you are meant to be doing. Doesn't our inner knowing tell us all the answers to the questions if we would only stop and listen.

How different would our lives be if we listened to our soul speaking to us every day through our heart and mind, and we made decisions about our day based on how we felt whilst living in a space of pure truth and honesty.

What would be your purpose and how would this affect your choice of career? Would you be living where you are now, or would you be somewhere else in the world? Are you happy with all your circumstances and if not, why not? And the grand daddy of all questions: Do you love yourself enough to give yourself all the things you need to be truly happy? Your soul knows the answers. All you need do is ask it the questions.

> *That which oppresses me, is it my soul
> trying to come out into the open,
> Or the soul of the world knocking
> at my heart for its entrance.*
>
> – RABINTRANATH TRAGORE

Upon setting sail to discover my most intimate thinking I began to write my thoughts down. I suggest you do the same for it is quite revealing. I asked myself all of the questions, that I have asked already and many more. It was the most interesting conversation with myself that I have ever had. I became my own therapist. This journaling was very personal and for my eyes only. It wasn't a lesson in editing, as it didn't matter what I wrote down as long as it was my truth. So don't be afraid to write down your thoughts for fear that someone might read what you have written. Even though it was personal, occasionally I shared my many revelations with people close to me. Often we laughed at my sillier ones.

This became a valuable assesment tool, once I unleashed a thought, put it on paper, then read it back to myself. Only then did I decide its validity. It is the easiest way I know to begin clearing away useless mind bog that takes up mental space, which we spend hours of our time thinking about. Buy a special journal and carry it with you as you never know when you'll have time or feel like writing.

I began by writing about my thoughts. Who I was, what I did, why I was doing it, how I was feeling and why I felt this way. I could see how my emotions had 'owned' my thinking for such a long time. I gave my hand the licence to free-think with my mind without judgement. I wrote whatever came into my head because this was pure thought.

It wasn't until later that I realised I was tapping into my very soul. To my astonishment, once I began I couldn't stop and found it easy to do. I had handed my spirit the key to my personal inner knowing about self. This was confronting and an exciting time — a revelation of personal truths. Only when I stopped and read what I had written did I understand its meaning. I was awakening my conscious mind with my unconscious thinking. Very powerful stuff when you first begin, but the moment you become aware of its importance and how it can affect your conscious awareness by bringing about change you will not want to stop.

Self realisation was fast becoming a religion for me and I spent many hours reading books that fueled my increasing thirst for knowledge. I delved into the very depths of my own mind, looking at some dark corners I didn't know existed for the first time.

> *The areas in your life where you find many insecurities, are your biggest and best teachers of self.*

I began to question my beliefs and their origin. Why did I think the way I did? I looked closely at patterns of behaviour that had occurred at different times in my life. For one reason or another I had many insecurities that I had quite cleverly covered up with other attributes of personality. I had always managed to give the impression that I had lots of confidence. Nothing could have been further from the truth. I was a master at disguise and I knew it.

When you start to challenge your own beliefs of self, born through the vehicle of experience, then you know you are on the right track. You are then in search of the real soul self. Who am I really? When you are confronted by who you really are and say to yourself, 'Gee this is who I am, but, it's not who I wish to be anymore,' then you are open and ready for some enlightenment.

I use to watch many movies years ago where the bad guy would do an about turn and do the right thing in the end by fixing his wrongs and winning back the heart of the people, only to die a martyr for the good of mankind.

I always thought that this has to be the most corniest, most untrue of endings. This could never really happen in real life! It never occurred to me that enlightenment could have taken place so that the villain had the opportunity to look at his behaviour and change within himself.

Although I always loved the ending, it sounded like a fairy tale for me at that time. Of course, I was wrong. It happens all the time, albeit in smaller ways. People are always changing within themselves. All too often we get stuck in our own beliefs. Now ready for change you seek tools for improvement.

> The most powerful thing you can do to change the world is to change your own beliefs about the nature of life, people, reality, to something more positive ...and begin to act accordingly.
> - SHAKTI GAWAIN.

I was to discover that quite a few of my beliefs about reality, life, people, etc., were born from mere fragments of information put together out of ignorance, and a deep desire to appear to have more knowledge than I did. I'm sure we have all been guilty of claiming to know more than we do. Newspapers do it all the time so why can't we! Slowly but surely more information would come to light and this would be added to the old information and updated. This is what they send us to school to learn. How to retain knowledge in our memory files to be used at a later date. It is the unfolding of our lives that keeps us in search for more information. We do not know it all yet and once you are aware of this process then you are slowly awakening to your own potential.

> When one realises one is asleep,
> at that moment one is already half-awake.
> - P.D. OUSPENSKY & G.I. GURDJIEFF.

How many times do you meet people who know it all. School is never out as long as you remain on the planet. Growth and learning are the very reasons that we incarnate so often. It is through the many lifetimes we experience what our soul's true purpose is as it becomes illuminated. While you are still alive you have work to do and personal growth is the labour no matter what form it takes.

Understanding the lessons

It is through the vehicle of cause and effect that we receive lessons and learn also about karma. Karma exists because of some action of non-forgiveness, debt or trauma, whether it be to self or another. To Buddhists this means the cosmic operation of retributive justice, according to which a person's status in life is determined by his own deeds in a previous life. For me I see it as inevitable consequence, or part of universal law.

For every cause there is an effect, so if your actions are of good cause then there will be good effect and therefore good karma. If you are coming from bad cause then there will be bad effect and bad karma. We are creating our own karma all the time. It pays to remember that what you give out to others and self you get back eventually in some form. Some karma appears in our life as patterns of behaviour and thought forms. To clear this kind of karma is simply a matter of letting go of these mental, emotional, or physical attachments to these patterns.

It matters not where you are at with learned knowledge or intellect. Everything works in keeping with your conscious awareness (your understanding of life). Your subconscious mind seeks out the lessons to bring your beliefs and karma into being, conscious. This gives you the chance to look at your beliefs and karma via circumstance. You then have an opportunity for growth through these circumstances with mind, body, emotions and soul.

What we learn from this is that we are totally responsible for what happens in our life. We are co-creators of our own reality, therefore, we cannot blame another for our response to an experience. As we evolve with our levels of awareness we learn how our beliefs, good and bad, positive and negative, become our reality. We can then choose the kinds of reality we wish to experience and get into flow with our living reality, creating better circumstances within our life. Sounds complicated but it's not really.

Before we can begin to understand any more about this we will have to look more closely at how we process information, on what levels we receive it and what we do with it. This will help us to understand why we think the way we do and how this processing of information relates to us our mental and emotional and ego self, to personality, our circumstances and karma. It will also explain why we receive lessons on the journey in search of soul's true purpose.

> **Child from Above**
> As we descend to the earth from the heavens above,
> we select our parents with the greatest of love.
> Unknown hosts for the beginning of life,
> they help give us shelter and keep us from strife.
> 'Tis an honour for them to give birth to our soul,
> and a blessing for us as we seek our life's goal.
> This love unconditional is a gift from your child,
> enjoy this love even when you are riled.
> Embrace your child with joy when they are near,
> feel your heart fill up and shed even a tear.
> When you are up in heaven viewing this child of love,
> you'll know that it came from the creator above.

The Four Levels

We are here to learn about self and we learn about self through four main channels of communication: the physical body, emotional body, mental body and its processes, and our spirituality.

Our lessons start from the moment we are born. We have already selected the time, place, parents and situation for this time around, best suited to the next stage in our spirit's growth. Yes, you do choose your parents. Hard to believe isn't it. You decide what situation is best suited for your growth in this life.

I believe that parents have some kind of karmic lessons for us in our life and it is up to us to grow from this. We know that family can play a big part in setting us up with personality and behavioural patterns for our future. Psychologists have been studying this for years.

Upon entering this physical dimension we undergo a kind of selected amnesia of our past lives and beyond. We have no memory as to why we are here, needless to say it is our soul's job to help us find our true self again whilst still in this human physical, emotional and mental world. We undergo many lessons of varying kinds, which gives us the opportunity to progress while clearing away karmic debt also.

Body
Physically through our bodies we experience appearance via image, diseases and our health, the effect of the atmosphere and living conditions, our body's strengths and its weaknesses, our sexuality, our gender, our colour and race, and the sensation of touch, physical pain and pleasure.

Emotions
Through our emotions we have experiences of a different nature such as, fear, resentment, anger, sadness, jealousy, loneliness, happiness, despair, nervous breakdowns, love, compassion, forgiveness, guilt, hate, depression, revenge and joy. We have an emotional reaction to all things that take place in our lives. However, we don't always acknowledge it.

Mind
Through the vehicle of our minds we experience all of the others in memory and such things as thoughts, learning, madness, genius, intellect, creativity, wonder, attitudes, paranoia, judgement, psychic abilities, mental defects, telepathy, our beliefs system, thought transformation and our connection to intuitive thinking. It's our computer for all data.

Spirit
On a spiritual plane we experience how we affect our world and learn to trust

our instinct through intuition while listening to our inner voices of conscience, honesty, compassion and truth for guidance. Learning and understanding our own spirituality is not about religion. It is about understanding self and how we affect others in our lives and taking these responsibilities to heart. Learning that love is what connects us all on the spiritual plane.

The life force and living spirit is everywhere. In the earth our living planet, in the stars and moon above, it's in the rivers and the seas, all plants and animals alike including humankind.

We learn that we are all nurtured by this force and that there is a connection between all living things. Some call it an energy, some call it God, some call it life force. I call it love, and it is all of these things.

This love energy is what drives us to learn about self for we need to learn to love self to pass through our barriers of fears and accept who we are completely and know that we are perfect already.

Personal spiritual growth seems to occur the more you share your own love energy with others. What you give out you get back. Your soul seeks out the right kind of spiritual growth that serves your purpose. If, however, you stray off the track for your spiritual growth then you will know when you have lost your way because you will have an overwhelming sense of discontent and life will be full of unhappiness.

Life will not be to your liking and because of this you will seek that which feeds your soul. It may be a place or person or a more creative self or job or environmental escape where you may think about self uninterrupted. Whatever you need to feed your soul and learn you will gravitate towards it eventually. Remember, all you need do is listen to your heart and your inner voices to be in touch with your soul.

The very reasons we seek answers from our soul about life and self is learning what it is that connects us all and how we fit into the scheme of things. Who we are and just what our true purpose is.

The Sea of Life

We are all connected by a magnificent force
felt as its ebb and flow floods our heart
with constant emotional waves of experience.
When the seas in your heart get stormy
drift with endurance and strength,
allowing understanding to fill your being
with love and trust, as our Soul has
the knowledge you'll need deep within.
As the navigator of this hearts life force
recognise your own wisdom and sail
on life's troubled waters with calm.
Only when you feel the current of life
pulling at your heart then it's time to
cast off and become one with it's source.
Enjoy each moment with love and happiness
as you celebrate the depths of each ocean
the heart will sail through
in the sea of life.

Chapter 2
Soul Verses Ego and Heart Verses Mind

How different would life be if every day, as the sun rose, we allowed ourselves to just be? If peace and harmony were the rule of the day, we would accept our birthright of personal growth to naturally take place. We could learn more about this from nature. For example: A plant does not need to think about its growth. Instead it accepts what influences this, like its supply of sun and water, it can expect a certain amount of growth per day, depending on the nutrients available from the soil. It is not in judgement of other plants around it because everything in nature is dependent on each other. So why is it that as humans we feel the need to be in judgement of each other's growth and even in competition for it?

What is Ego?

We do not grow any faster than is necessary and we do not experience anything we cannot handle. Everything works in keeping with our own conscious awareness, so it is an unnecessary behaviour for us to compete. But to feed the ego and seek out our limits, compete we must. We can see how our personality takes shape as our ego challenges our nature throughout our life. You were not created with a personality; it is an ego-born event.

So what is ego? Part of ego is our vanity shown and reflected to others in the judgements and attitudes we adopt for the obtaining of validation, power and influence over others. Ego seeks constant validation of our physical and emotional reasons for being and seeks to set us apart from others. Ego can be seen as ambition and a consciousness of self, the person we wish others to see instead of the person we really are. Ego is what makes women wear make-up masks that totally changes their real image instead of only enhancing it. Ego is what makes men boast about their sexual pursuits to each other.

Ego is what makes us think we are either totally unacceptable or better than anyone else. Personality is what we project to others, it is the external self, shaped by our ego and can be changed and moulded as you grow with your external experience of life. Harnessed correctly it can be put to good use with your future pursuits.

Like a river winding to meet the sea so shall your understanding of self expand and flow. The personality takes shape and is developed by response from the messages you receive via emotional and behavioural patterns you learn, along with the mental attitudes you have come to adopt as a result. So your personality is by no means fixed in concrete. When people say they cannot change, it isn't because they can't, it is because they don't want to; their ego won't let them.

Competition

In almost all areas of our lives we compete in some form or other. We judge ourselves on how other's behave, by what they have in their possession, how they come by them and by the responses these things get from others. Our judgmental ego lets us believe that we also must have these possessions to be equal and this is why we compete.

> **Ego Performs**
> Ego is a menace, which influences our thoughts
> for attentions and validation of various sorts.
> To receive recognition and for friends to stay
> 'tis ego which performs and helps win the day.
> It lies to our heart about what is true,
> it inflates its growth to others about you.
> We should not allow the ego to control,
> but in life it has purpose and a role.
> To look past our emotional wants and needs
> and see a higher purpose for our life deeds.
> When ego is conquered and soul exposed
> the ego will no longer seek to impose.
> For it has learned from lessons committed
> that life is love shared and must be permitted.
> Acceptance of all, rules out competition
> but ego quite often will need this tuition.

As youngsters we competed for love, with our sisters and brothers, for our mother's or father's affections. Needing approval and love and validation as children we sometimes seek it through other means, especially if our parents are too busy with their lives.

Competition is easily recognisable in the school yard. It is the way we first try to obtain recognition and acceptance from peers and friends.

As youngsters we enjoy sporting activities with each other. However, when we realise that we can receive recognition for winning in this arena it takes on a whole new meaning. This can set up the belief in children that on a physical level we can be better than another person, because our peers say so and reward this. Children see this reward as validation, attention, and recognition sometimes as replacement for the love they believe they are not getting at home.

New levels of self awareness are set up within a child and that is where competition can feed the ego. Those who excel in this area test their limits constantly, believing that to get rewarded they have to be the best, perform regularly and do better.

Personalities take form and so egos are fueled and this sometimes gives flight to boasting behaviour. Making oneself better than someone else, or right and the other person wrong or not as good as, is how we falsely increase our energy by stealing someone else's. This is the very basis of most of our ego battles and wars by making one person better than another or seeing one as strong and the other as weak.

Children who are not good in one area, physically, usually seek out another one to prove that they are just as good. This behaviour gives rise to the many different kinds of sporting activities we see today. You only have to see the hundreds of sporting events now in the Olympics. You can see how we use these sporting heroes as icons of our society and how they are worshipped and financially rewarded.

Schools have set up reward systems for academics in all areas so that other children are not left out. Not everyone feels the need to compete at school. Somewhere in our life we usually seek recognition, and competition usually plays a part. This could be in business, with love life or career or in the acquisition of material wealth.

Knowledge and Ego

We have, for one reason or another, sought mountains to climb, with our egos leading the way. For whatever the reason, we seek, for our personality's sake, validation on all levels. None more so than with the acquisition of knowledge.

Mentally, people have challenged themselves and so seek out huge amounts of knowledge, with some spending many years of their lives at universities. There seems to be a need to obtain more and more degrees and letters after our name. I have met many people who have heaps of book knowledge but who have difficulty in accepting change or making a decision in their lives, simply because of the fears that they have neglected to challenge in reality due to their continual study. It is a form of intellectual escape from reality.

I have enjoyed many interesting conversations with university graduates of an absorbing nature, only for them to ask what university I had attended. Astonished at this I laughingly said that I had attended the 'University of Life', exposing to them their intellectual snobbery and misconception that intelligence and intellect went hand in hand with a degree. Of course this is incorrect, intelligence has not a lot to do with intellect, rather it is a more common sense approach to life, using correctly what knowledge one has at the time.

> *Being intelligent is not being studious.*
> *It is knowing how to be fulfilled*
> *in all circumstances.*

Knowledge of all sorts has been stolen, copied, lied about and cheated for, all in the name of ego, wanting to be as good as, and better than the next person. Knowledge for knowledge sake is useless unless it is used for action in some way. Don't get me wrong, I am not condemning universities. They have their place in society and this type of thinking is healthy because it means that in the short term you may challenge yourself which will result in growth. When your ego becomes useful to your soul's growth it works for you and not against you. Most events born of ego end up consuming themselves and burning out.

To continually be in competition is to falter at some stage, allowing your personality the chance to look at itself through some kind of personal failure. Thinking that something is wrong it now looks for other ways to project success so as to feel validated again and feed the ego some more. We continue with this dance until we realise that pursuit of success for success is not validating. It leaves you empty and drained wondering why you bothered in the first place. We become bored, discontented and feel empty with our achievements, realising that they no longer feed the soul. However, ego keeps looking for new proving grounds for success to feel recognition and validation again.

> *Only then do we understand that our success lies in the intentions of our deeds, which in turn will give our life purpose.*

On the physical level those who spend a lifetime punishing their body with sport end up with very sore and burnt out bodies with many complaints that doctors would be only to happy to share with you. Our body was meant to be exercised, yes, but continually abused, no. Our soul has no use for a worn out body. What purpose could it have with this; the body expires and the soul moves on.

Mentally, it is great to have plenty of knowledge if you get to make use of it. Hiding behind a mountain of books, afraid to come out is not healthy; it limits your experience of life. Your soul only has use for knowledge if you are prepared to store it for future reference and use it for your spirit's growth and highest purpose.

It is necessary to find a purpose for living and when we connect with our soul we start to listen to our heart's desires. Wishing to serve this inner person we seek to move on from the struggle of survival. Now we wish to be of use to the community so we seek out our true purpose. Knowing this the inner person begins to want to project success; the choices made then are crucial.

You can then use the developed personality or ego's drive and ambition for a much higher purpose. Ego's drive and need for validation and success can be used to profit everybody, including you. As you learn to make decisions for your physical world based on your inner world's desires, you are then changing the very nature of your outer experience with inner self (*or soul*) instead of the ego's external personality and need for validation.

Crisis resulting from this is an opening for spiritual growth because you are no longer wanting to live just to support your life's external ego needs. Soul is exposed and listened to, ego is conquered and put aside for now, waiting until doubt creeps in so that it can rear again its head. This battle between soul and ego will go on for some time until you go through a period of unlearning the ego's false responses of validation or success.

Each time you manage to put your self back on track, aligning with your soul, you'll feel elated and seek more of this feeling. Each time ego takes over you are reminded of the false illusions of success it sets up and how it is never satisfied. Empty and depleted you return to self for the answers in search of soul. Wondrous things happen when ego is finally wrestled with and the soul is set free.

And My Soul Spoke

To follow my heart and set it free,
to lead my life and find true destiny.
To allow myself to be and share this with another,
to heal my soul with an unconditional lover.
To find my way in this world today.
Ah, to go, to be free to fly away.

God, I don't know where I would start,
perhaps visiting family and lost loves of heart.
Perhaps I'd find peace in the earth's terrain,
out west on the coast in the mountains or plains.
Anywhere my heart and soul wish to be,
To sing, to dance, to laugh and play free.

But what of money and possessions you say.
They do not feed my heart and soul this way.
I see this as baggage we drag along.
My heart and soul don't need this to feel strong.
Love of self is all that I need,
to no longer feel the lure for greed.

To help with the evolvement of the human race,
to use all for the betterment of our time and space.
To see and explore all that life has to offer
is to be blessed in this life and live it proper.
So my soul speaks to me through my heart,
if I ask will it know where I am to start?

To not feel alone in my world anymore,
to seek out with vengeance all this and more.
What next you ask, is this woman mad?
No I say, just inside she is sad

at the trouble I've made out of my life.
'Twas my ego that's caused all of this strife.
Living for false cause can inflict pain,
not living in truths so I still remain.
Here in this rut I call circumstance,
can't I just get up, leave, take a chance.

What would happen if I dared to take flight.
Well, I don't know, maybe you're right.
If my heart and soul had their way
in this place I would not want to stay.
Do I trust in life to be there for me,
shall I take the next step to my destiny?
Sometimes it's through fear of the unknown
we experience the failure of illusions we're shown.

Do I listen to the voice that says this is wrong?
Do I face the choice to take courage, be strong?
It would be a brave thing to do to just walk away
with the knowledge that life would support my stay.
I know what I'm doing serves no purpose right now,
but patience is a virtue and I'm learning how.
To use it well in this, God's garden I'm waiting
with my heart and soul still contemplating.

We have all been told not to follow our heart for it leads us astray and does not keep us in control. Nothing could be further from the truth. When you follow your heart you are in fact in control, being true to self and not allowing ego's intellectual commonsense to reign.

> When you deny the yearnings of the heart you deny the wishes of the soul.

Heart versus Mind

Because of our negative programming we question the heart's desires and the 'heart verses mind battle' goes something like this: Is this right for me? Do I need this? Is it going to be hard to do? Can I afford this? We justify and rationalise our thinking, believing that our heart is deceiving us, when, in fact, it is the messenger of your soul's desires in this life. This is a difficult battleground for us because our external needs are important and can dictate what we decide, especially if it is in opposition to our heart's desires. So the conflicts get very complicated when heart verses mind. Your survival of this battle will then lead to the biggest doorway for the soul to enter. Your soul talks through the heart but ego comes through the mind.

> We should make decisions from the heart only and let the mind work it into our reality via action.

A funny thing happens when the heart aligns with the soul. You make decisions with more integrity, using your mind with dexterity. We spend a lot of time fine tuning our minds with knowledge from schools and the like so we cannot dismiss it's valid thinking and we must respect it too. So where does this leave us in our conflict and how should we handle this? The pathway to the soul is through the heart. It is through the using of the heart for decisions that who you really are is exposed to you as well as others. Through this doorway you will begin to realise that it is not enough to just delve into the depths of the mind. Now you need to work on the mind and the heart together.

You will learn about your own integrity and gain mental and emotional dexterity with your decision-making process by walking the path of self honour and self honesty. This is where soul enters our life and we start on our spiritual inner quest for the right answers. We look for a more profound meaning to life. This is why we need to align with our soul and heart because they never lie.

We begin to realise that a large house is not necessary for us to live in to be happy. That lots of money is great but does not love us or keep us company. That a job that keeps us too busy, separating us from the ones we love so that we lose touch with them, is not working for us. That to be happy in whatever you are doing feels good and right. When we stop and listen to our heart, life takes on a whole new meaning. We get real about our priorities and align with our true purpose and soul.

At this time real purpose for our life becomes an important issue. It is then that our soul goes in search of this true purpose. Now we can look at our life and begin to understand who we are and what it is we could be doing with what we have learnt. Finding the balance between needs, desires, purpose and destiny in our life is important to our well-being. Balancing what we can already do with what we would like to be doing is the key to freedom. This is the period where we look at the things we have to do in order to survive and the things we would like to be doing for our real purpose and try to marry the two in reality. For a time we struggle with the impending difficulties while looking at ways to change our existing situations, especially if it's not already working for us.

You open up to guidance from your intuition and inner feelings by using the mind's resources of knowledge and our soul's wisdom,.

> *Understanding the path of the soul is like Luke Skywalker in 'Star wars'. You give your heart and soul the reigns and fly by the seat of your pants, using the Force and your intuition to carry you forward.*

Your soul has the memory of all your past experiences and the knowledge within them. From these you can gain an understanding of just what your life purpose is this time around. For some of you this is something you may not be sure about; however, you may want to recall some of the events that have shaped your life. Sometimes we deny ourselves the very thing that has been knocking on our door for some time. I personally know people who went out and became mechanics early in their lives, only to eventually become teachers and trainers as they were led to purpose.

You know when the mind and common sense has taken over your heart's desires because it fills your head with justification and guilt and all sorts of confused thoughts. One friend who became a mechanic did so because his father told him he had to have something to fall back on in life. It took him a long time of trial and error before he admitted to himself he was not happy. It wasn't until someone else put him in charge of teaching others that his real talents were shown to him.

> *Doing what you love is the cornerstone to having abundance in your life.*

My advice to you is if your head becomes clouded and you cannot think anymore or you just wish it to stop, then sit back relax, maybe meditate, do nothing, or do something else, but shift focus. Allow things to settle in your mind and when you are calm and peaceful then ask your heart what it really wants and listen. Don't worry, this is a classic sign that decision is on its way, and out of confusion comes choice; funny enough it seems we all go through this type of process with our heart verses mind battles.

There will be your true answers. Even if they are difficult to admit to yourself or to others, you will know that they are ultimately what you wish to do, so do it. Start and put it into place in your living reality. This could take time, so remember, Rome wasn't built in a day.

> *When the heart verses the mind 'tis our soul's crossroad for growth.*

Weeding the path

The heart and mind conflict becomes very hard when it involves loved ones or personal relationships that are in the way of your soul's desires for growth. The heart has a tough time with this as it seems to split into two: the things our soul wants verses our emotional needs.

There is a third player in this battle and that is the commitments you have made due to circumstances either mental, emotional or financial. It is these commitments that we find hard to free ourselves of, but believe me, doing so will eventually feel like the shedding of an artificial skin. Once you can release yourself from these the pathway to what you are wanting to take place can happen. I call this time 'weeding the path.'

Before you commit to anything new, take into consideration what your purpose and goals are and remember them. Then ask yourself is what you are about to commit yourself to going to help work towards these goals. If, in the long run, it's not helpful, then I would think very seriously about making any commitment at all. Sure, help out if you like, but make no commitments, keep your ultimate goals in mind. Often it's these continual side tracks in circumstance, that stop us from seeking and finding our purpose and allowing us to get on with it.

All this can be seen very clearly with the bringing up of teenagers. This is a joyous time in our lives. However, it can reach a stage where their very presence causes tension and conflict as they grow up. The fact is that on a soul level they are not aligned with the parent anymore and need to find their own path. They rebel trying to find a way out.

For their own growth they need to separate from their parent's influences, even though these come from love. This kind of mind and heart conflict is complicated and when you have deliberated over this you will come to the conclusion that your needs are important and your life must continue. As parents our true purpose sometimes gets lost in the raising of children and we need to learn about selfless unconditional love through parenting for growth. Quite often parent and child part at this time so each may experience growth on an emotional, financial, physical and spiritual level.

Family can also be the weeds in your pathway and so must be removed with loving guidance. If this happens, then it is in their highest good and quite correct for you also. Both can move forward on their soul's quest when released from the emotional battles. The relationship between parent and child will come back into being more loving when the child reaches a more mature level of understanding and growth and the parent can accept the child's right to individuality. Of course, not all children are experienced this way. I have two daughters that could not have been more different as they grew up. It pays to remember that we as parents cannot put an old head on young shoulders. They must grow at their own pace and be allowed to make their mistakes as we did. We should not be in judgement of this.

Children need to learn that parents are people just like themselves and they too deserve respect on their life's path. This particular conflict is common now as I have spoken to many parents everywhere. I believe this is because there has been a quickening in our children's consciousness as our lives are speeding up.

They are experiencing growth much earlier than before and are more accepting and aware than we ever were and grow up faster as a result. They have no need for our outdated thinking. However, some of the values will still need to be taught. Some still choose to learn the hard way. That is their choice and we must allow it.

> We are now discovering
> that it is okay to be who we need to be,
> and to let others be who they need to be also.

Now that you know how the soul, ego, heart and mind battle it out within you it will be much easier for you to understand the processes that take place. Learning to listen to them all will tell you just where your head is at and how your heart feels about it while the soul sits back trying to stop our ego from getting in the way too much.

Learning to use all the positive attributes of personality for the right purpose is always satisfying, but initially a little illusive. You will want to find your purpose enough to ask the right questions and you will be guided to do this. Trusting your heart will become second nature once you have felt the positive results it can achieve.

Once you give it wings to fly your whole existence takes on a new journey. This will prove to be most satisfying and beneficial to you. The places you will go and the people you will meet in the future will surprise you and delight you. Don't be too hard on yourself. Remember one day at a time.

Open Heart

> Our heart is the place that our mind reconciles
> with the love that we feel for one another.
> 'Tis the core of our being and our engine for life
> that we open to greet each other.
> When the soul and the heart align this journey
> It's much easier to travel along.
> Your heart always knows where it's going
> but the ego and mind think it's wrong.

*The heart helps shine a light on your pathway
with use this will soon become bright.
May your heart stay on track through the dark
so it leads you back to the light.*

IN SEARCH OF SOUL

Chapter 3
Castle of our Mind

In the search for soul we come across a large castle within self. It is guarded well with high barriers put in place by the ego. One day the need is so great that we move past the barriers, dissolving the ego walls, knowing there is something here worth discovering. This castle is the castle of our mind and is sacred with its knowledge of the self.

Encased behind the castle wall lies many secrets of our being. To travel through its many corridors, unlocking secret doors to passages that lead to either the dark dungeons or open courtyards of your mind is your mission at the moment. Learning to understand how, from your main chamber of thought, you are led down a number of passages to choices. You then turn these choices into action which lead to the many circumstances you find in your life. Thoughts, decisions and choices lead to action. This is how the castle works.

It is quite simple. There can be no action without first there having been a thought from whence it came. The body does not act on its own. It must have a directive from your mind. Your mind is the castle and thought is the nerve centre or main chamber of operation. Accepting the mental and emotional responsibilities of our actions has long been a battleground for many a novice warrior beginning to learn about self.

I have found that blame and denial is their main barrier or escape within their mind. However, we eventually all learn in the end and everyone learns at their own pace. Learning about the mind and its processes may seem slow. You may want to help others along but it will not make any difference. It will only serve for frustration on both sides.

We all need to be patient in our getting of wisdom. The maze of processes you need to understand at this point in time can take a whole lifetime to unravel. Life is like a long twisted rope, untying many knots along the way.

As each knot is approached, like the many difficulties we experience, you find yourself getting frustrated and angry until you allow this lack of self love to dissolve, so that frustration can be replaced with caring and calm, nurturing yourself with patience and compassion, so all is unraveled with ease. The mere mention of the word patience sends everyone looking for the shortest route, rarely is it the fastest. How long does it take for us to learn this?

> *Those who think that the world is a dark place are blind to the light that might illuminate their lives*

Hearing self talk

Learning about how our mind works takes patience, so don't be too hasty or hard on yourself. So where do we begin?

Very simply you begin by listening to the things you say to others. Begin by listening to your own conversations and learn to be mindful. Hear your beliefs, dreams and desires. While listening to your self talk do you turn all conversation back to self or do you listen to what is really being said? Do you say things just to get a reaction and attention? Ask yourself would you like what you have just said repeated back to you. Listen to your beliefs and think about their origin. If you hear yourself say something you don't like then realise you are becoming more tuned in.

Upon tuning into your self talk you may recognise some faults and not like what you hear yourself say. Being mindful and taking heed of your conversation is a responsible pathway to growth of this kind. I feel it would be much better to discover something I don't particularly like about my thinking from myself than wait to be told by another. We don't always like to be told. This can be clearly felt when hearing yourself voice a criticism to someone about someone else. Listen to your criticism of others and ask how you would feel if that was said about you. Are you voicing this out of concern for their life or safety or is it just plain faultfinding? Listening to yourself criticising is the beginning of some deep healing because we usually see in others aspects we dislike about self.

The same could be said when we discredit another person's right to an opinion or a belief. Making judgements states to others that you have a closed mind and suffer with rigid thinking, not allowing others to have separate ideas to yours. This is a human failing and has been the eternal inner struggle with humankind seeking to steal another person's power by making self right and the others wrong.

Being in judgement of others because they either say or do something different to the way you would is making them wrong and you right.

For whatever reason this is our biggest global problem. It exists in our religions, our beliefs of ownership, our relationships between the races and the sexes and between the old and the new. Unfortunately, judgement is the basis of laws that govern the judicial systems in every culture and country. We have been mentally battling it out since Adam was a boy.

Letting go of the need of expectations of others and the 'right and wrong' belief systems seems hard at first. Accepting and allowing everything sounds idealistic and not attainable. It is quite simple. It lies simply in the act of letting go of old belief patterns and outdated and out-moded thinking.

> *Any belief you hold onto stands in your pathway to growth*

Learning to take heed of your own judgements is the beginning of a huge healing process towards the acceptance of self and others. With acceptance in our hearts we no longer need to control or change self or others anymore. When, as a human race, we can collectively let go of judgement then we can begin to live together again in acceptance, peace and harmony.

Judgement

As a child our world around us
was safe and loving and kind.
'Tis harsh when we learn from our peers
and their judgements are what we find.
We journey to this place not knowing
that it's self we are here to discover.
Judgement is a veil of learning
we help to lift from one another.
Try to see past all our differences,
understand none of us are the same.
There's no need for ignorant judgements
so let go of the need for blame.
For in the end it is judgement of self
that inhibits growth on the whole.
When we release the judgements of others
it's acceptance we receive from soul.

The Mirrors of Life

During the course of my life I have met many people who were there to help teach me through love and gentle guidance, although at the time I was unaware of them doing so. They presented themselves as friends during some of my most difficult mental and emotional lessons. It was their unconditional love and support I could not have done without. They gave freely of their time for those many hours of discussion which took place, helping me make a monumental decision that changed the course of my life.

We all have these kinds of teachers along the way. They will give you the validation and space to be as screwed up as you like at that particular time in your life. Without judgement they will support you in your hour of most need and the memory of this will touch your heart and soul in such a way that you will never want to forget them.

Like me you will vow and declare that you'll keep in touch with them for always and they quite often become your truest friends. Their deeds and their wisdom lingers on when they have gone. Some of us are blessed with this kind of teacher or friend as a parent or brother or sister.

I was to discover that my own mother was just such a person. Only after she left my father and was true to herself could she give me the support and unconditional love that I had craved and needed for so long.

If you are fortunate enough you may even marry just such a person whom you will love and cherish all of your life as a true soulmate. I have been blessed with some lovely friends along my journey. Some of them are unaware of their influence upon me only because I have not seen them for many years.

Sometimes it is the negative things we see in others that makes us decide we do not want to project that kind of situation to everyone else. I have tried to live by the standard of doing unto others as I would like done to me. Sounds corny but it works.

What I like most about friends is the fact that they are mirrors of self so if you don't like some of your friends it is because they mirror a part of you that you are not looking at but need to address. Don't waste time trying to fix others, just love and support them, they will find their way.

To be surrounded by good friends is to be surrounded by your own good qualities reflected in others. This mirroring effect can be seen in our love relationships as well.

Friends

The friends we meet through our life as we travel,
these relationship journeys allow us to unravel,
the experience of people strange places and more,
'tis your inner feelings friends help you explore.
Strangers are but friends you haven't met yet,
fear of them would serve only for your regret.
A friend indeed will be what you will find,
when you open your heart and open your mind.
Don't judge others, we are all different you'll see,
instead, sing, laugh and enjoy their company.

The Emotional Chambers

Understanding the castles of your mind is about looking at the way you think and what patterns or habits this can create. I have found that most people think with their emotions first. They either can't or don't wish to evaluate information properly before they answer or react. Running conversation by your emotions can have an amazing effect on your reactions.

When someone is talking to you, do you take what they are saying on board personally and get offended by a mere comment? If you find this happening to you then realise the problem could be in your translation or reaction of the information given to you. If you are feeling at all insecure then it is easy to be upset or offended by mere comments. Possibly, your knowledge of the person is limited or you may not have liked the way they spoke to you and so feel a little threatened by them, or maybe you were intimidated by anyone with knowledge that you did not have at that time.

These things are very common human failings with communication — feeling the information instead of listening to it in its true context. I found this to be part of my own problem years ago when I was starting to learn something.

I would focus on my own lack of confidence only to feel insecure, which meant that I was unable to comprehend the information due to the fact that I had already decided emotionally that I could not possibly understand it as I was not clever enough. Immediately I was intimidated. Fear stepped in and I was terrified that I would be asked a question I could not possibly answer, making learning a stressful experience.

All of this mind bog meant in reality that I robbed myself of the opportunity to learn what I was being told, only confirming my belief that I was not clever. Emotions and fears immobilise us and steal our personal power and growth. These fears I had were born out of not feeling I was good enough and that everyone else was better and knew more than I did. A typical insecure state of being. I eventually learned that to open myself up to receiving information led to a growth in my understanding.

> You are not stuck unless you decide to be.

If you really wish to learn something you will conquer your fears and emotions. This was how I learnt to expose my feelings. I did this by admitting first to myself and then to others how I felt. Telling people I was anxious and nervous helped me to come to terms about my fear.

Others would share with me their feelings of nervousness as well making me realise I was not alone. Sometimes it pays to be honest and open. Instead of hiding your insecurities learn to expose them and you will find that they disappear almost immediately. I know that this can be hard when you first start exposing any insecurity, but the more you trust that most people wish to help you the more you will feel comfortable about doing this.

It is not a sin to feel insecure with a lack of some knowledge. Insecurity is your mind letting you know that new information is presenting itself and that an opportunity now exists for growth. It is a challenge sometimes to open the mind without fear.

Impostor

Fear is the only thing that gets in the way,
obstructing the flow of our life's play.
Future thoughts bring a stream of confusion
with which we draw a fearful conclusion.
These fears are born from an ignorant source.
'Tis the ego trying to control our course.
They are but illusions soon you'll see,
this maze of thoughts you'll chart to be free.
So stretch beyond the things you know.

> *In life, trust is an exercise in letting go.*
> *Once fears are conquered and then exposed*
> *for the impostors they are when the mind is closed.*
> *You'll see the growth that you may obtain,*
> *so on your life's path you now will remain.*

Memory

The castle of your mind has many files and categories for memory. The memory of people, your responses to them and the reactions felt by these encounters. It is the same for places you go to and the experiences you have there. The mind remembers everything that happens in your life. It registers the thoughts, opinions and feelings you have had in the past. It is all divided up and digested for analysis, slotted into files and used in future thought as your personal backup system.

This, of course, goes on in your subconscious mind all the time. Even during dreams you are only trying to make sense of everything your mind has registered during the day. Dreams seem to play an important role in clearing away mental debris. When all else fails we use the memory of past events to predict the future. This can be good in some situations, especially when safety is needed or a learned skill is recalled. However, when dealing with our emotions it tends to cloud our judgement of a person or place or experience, depending on a particular past experience. We even base some of our own judgements on other people's emotional past experiences.

Others can influence our thinking where our emotions are concerned. The power of projected negative emotions from others is very strong, especially if they are family or a close relationship. Realising now that you have some serious decisions to make, like who controls your thoughts emotionally? Do you let others think for you? I hope not, for no one thinks for you but you.

The memory of a negative emotion can close us off to a new feeling or experience that would otherwise have been enjoyed if it wasn't for that memory stepping in to haunt us. For some unknown reason we seem to collect, enlarge and distort more of the negative emotions to memory. So fear becomes a huge player in our responses to most levels of information. To understand fear you need to also understand emotions. Our emotions give us choice by helping us feel our way.

> ### Emotions
>
> When we face the things that have caused us pain,
> we then face the choices of returning to them again.
> Our emotions are but feelings we need to trust,
> and know that these lessons in our life are a must.
> To see fears are but reflections of failure unknown,
> and guilt is our conscience not wanting to come home.
> That resentment is the anger we felt so long ago,
> and bitterness is forgiveness not wanting to let go.
> Know that anger we all feel when life we can't control,
> and loneliness is longing for love of self from soul.
> But happiness is the place we all long to be,
> and joy is the glow of sheer bliss and harmony.
> Love is the space in our hearts we will find,
> soul manifests through the vehicle of our mind.

Emotions

Emotions are a barometer of how we feel about something. To deny your emotions is to not acknowledge your real feelings. Some of us deny our own emotional truths and live in personal lies, fearful of the real 'us' being exposed. Emotions are messages from the soul's memory and it is okay to have them and to express them. You can intellectualise your emotions with knowledge. However, if you do not accept them and do not do something about how you feel, nine times out of ten you'll regret it. Emotions give you the opportunity to look at yourself a little more deeply, especially when you look at their origin of why we feel the way we do.

Some of our emotional responses come from our beliefs about self. These are put together from the positive and negative programming we receive from very early in our life. But it is the negative responses that get the most air play in your mind.

Fear is self doubt on any level and, of course, is expressed as a negative emotion. I was always told that fear was **F**alse **E**vidence **A**ppearing **R**eal. Conclusions of a future we knew nothing about. These false conclusions jaundice our mind and stop us from having new experiences. Do you need to consult an imaginary, fear-based history to make real-life decisions. This is easy to see when we look at personal love lives of those who have been hurt. They are quite often emotionally wounded for some time unable to allow themselves to love again until they recover, believing that the negative emotion they experienced happens when in love.

Nevertheless, I had a hard time learning to deal with my emotional fears. I was definitely a warrior fighting them off in full armor, battle shield and sword.

> *The fastest way to freedom is to feel your feelings.*
> – Gita Bellin

Love and Fear do Battle

There are many different kinds of fear but they all have one thing in common, they are all illusions that we bring forth due to a negative belief. The cure for all fears, no matter what it is, is very simply love. Love and fear cannot dwell in the same space. A love thought is the most powerful thought you can manifest in the mind. It has the power to turn everything around.

If you are in doubt about this try this exercise when you are angry. Ask yourself in full flight of anger whether you are coming at that person or situation from a space of love or fear. Looking more closely at thought now you will see, that there are only two types of thought: one is based on fear and the other is based on love. Think about this. I guarantee that you will find that anger is born out of the fear of not being able to control that other person or circumstance. To combat this you need to love the situation and trust that whatever is happening is for a reason and you do not need to interfere or direct it. Trust in life and let it be.

As a parent I have personally tested this one a lot with my teenage daughter. I have been able to diffuse many arguments by simply reminding myself to come from a space of love for her and release the need to control her behaviour or mind with my expectations. The biggest insult you can give another person is to try and impose your thinking onto them. Being angry because someone did not do what we expected of them or because they do not see what we mean is a form of fear and control. We can only ever try to influence others with our suggestions. The choice always remains within an individual.

A true master of a person's mind waits to be asked a question before giving of their wisdom. Respect is thereby maintained with the exchange between teacher and pupil, the parent and child and between friends.

> We are all free to be
> who we wish to be.

When we are intimidated or interrogated by peers or parents we either resent what they have said or we feel guilty for not conforming to their wishes or beliefs. Guilt, if it is allowed to build up in your life, becomes your automatic, emotional response to many situations and leaves you weak, especially when you say sorry for your very being.

When feeling vulnerable you can be used because you want desperately to please everyone, allowing this at the expense of self. For some this was the only way they got positive attention as a child. These people find it hard to say no and so their conscience becomes so weighted down with guilt that they suppress all their own needs constantly, believing that to get recognition they must please others always and deny the self.

'Twas Conscience

The guilt that I've felt in my life from the past
was born of false cause I've realised at last.
'Twas conscience tricked into feeling the blame
by events that were twisted from whence they came.
Our conscience measures selfishness for sure,
'tis answers for selfish others I seek no cure.
A martyr I'll become if this turns into behaviour,
it's guilt that becomes our slave or our saviour.
When it returns home conscience will be strong,
for it knows the difference between right and wrong.
This will be a test that I have to tend
with strength I'll know less of guilt in the end.

Women over the centuries have felt guilty due to the fact that society had made them subservient to men. This I am happy to see is finally being lifted from the female consciousness, opening the doorway for love of the feminine principal. Respect for each other in both of the sexes is returning at last. Guilt stops others from seeing that they are responsible for their actions. You have no need to take the blame for their lacking.

Many people suffer with long standing negative emotions such as guilt, rendering themselves weak which results in illness. They end up with cancer and tumours and breakdowns as a result. Sad isn't it? The cancer or the breakdown then becomes the catalyst for them to look at themselves and learn about life from a whole new perspective. They then begin to ask the questions that leads to their pilgrimage in search of soul.

Sometimes it takes trauma of the mind for people to move into that space which helps them to receive enlightenment of self. A little drastic but very common. Only then are they open for the right information and so when the pupil is ready the teachers will be found and the lessons presented.

Learning how our mind works is just one of the ways to understanding self. If you can master your mind then you can begin to master your emotions and represent yourself much more truly to others, no longer fearful of their responses. You now accept and understand that they are totally responsible for their own beliefs and their reactions also.

All this knowledge helps empower you to grow in your own conscious awareness. Learning about your mind helps you take responsibility for everything you do in your life.

There will be times that you have to remind yourself of something about your beliefs or thinking, but you will get better at this the more you practice. This kind of awareness is ongoing as life does not stand still. Be prepared to update any beliefs at will as they will be challenged throughout your life.

Creating choices

As we journey through life we have many choices to make. Some of these choices are easy while others are more complicated. As a seeker of self one of the hardest things for me to take responsibility for were my choices. These took the forms of all the experiences I helped co-create, the many perceptions I made and the beliefs I had.

First I was in denial of having anything to do with creating those areas of my life that I was not happy with. I had to realise that I placed myself in these predicaments with the people that brought about the unhappy circumstances, so in this way I must have had a hand in co-creating the events.

This was a huge revelation about the choices I had made and it helped me to realise that if I could make some bad choices then maybe I could make some good choices as well. Especially if I looked closer at the mind I felt it would improve my understanding of people and circumstances. I became more aware of my thinking habits and the patterns these created. I then analysed the habit to understand where it came from. I asked myself which part of me was creating this habitual thought. First, I would establish what sort of thought I was having; was it a happy thought, was it an ego thought, was it an emotional thought? If it was, which emotion was it?

Writing things down helped me look at this more closely. Most of my thoughts were based on a feeling of some kind. Once I could establish this feeling or emotion then I would ask myself was it correct for me to feel that way or not. Realising that these feelings are only thoughts and thoughts can be changed, I then could change this thought or any other thoughts that were not from good feelings.

Sounds a bit complicated? But it all happens within our minds in a matter of seconds once we have learnt it and got past the mechanical process of learning it. Learning to change negative thought patterns became a real challenge for me. Taking the responsibility for your own choices about your feelings means that you can no longer blame another person for your feelings. They don't make you think you are hurting — you do! Your feelings are simply a response and you choose that response.

You are totally responsible for your own reactions to any life experience. There is no right or wrong way to experience anything. An experience is just that, an experience. If you didn't like your reaction then change it. The mind if used wisely can be your best friend all of the time. However, if you continually program it negatively it can be your worst enemy, defeating your very purpose.

> You have the choice continually with how you wish to be, only you can make a difference to your thinking.

All external things can only influence this. They are not the blame. Looking at yourself more closely now you will see that you are totally responsible for all of your thinking and how this effects you in future experiences.

Who is Responsible?

Learning about responsibility will be given to you in many ways. Some will learn through their careers by taking on many tasks and proving that they can handle them. Responsibility can be found almost in any situation that requires you to exist. Simply living requires you to pay the rent or mortgage, telephone and electricity bills, as well as keep house and self clean and tidy. If you have children and a job of some kind then the responsibilities increase. What and how you learn from these experiences will depend on how you handle the responsibility.

So many people find being responsible a hard lesson and have it repeated many times before they are prepared to accept it. Once we can accept responsibility for others and their well-being then we take responsibility for self as a matter of course. What we have learned to do quite simply is to trust ourselves to do what is right and cope no matter what. We learn to wear the consequences of our decisions about what we are responsible for. Responsibility is about being mindful of choices and their effect on self, others and circumstance.

Trusting self is an act of self confidence and self love and can only be achieved through trial and error during the course of your life. When you start to trust self you start to believe in self and you begin to trust in life also. You grow up and see how things work in the real world. Trust is a leap in consciousness and responsibility.

> ### Trust
>
> Trust is something we earn from each other,
> it cannot be borrowed or lent to a brother.
> To know honour and loyalty then understand,
> you are blessed with trust on this great land.
> Trust is knowing your heart is true,
> the deeds you perform will reflect this too.
> When your ego is conquered and soul exposed,
> 'tis trust of self you'll seek unopposed.

Early in my life I have had lots of responsibilities placed on me, more than my share I thought. This has made me a dependable employee with the confidence to embark on my own businesses later on. I was able to accept all of the responsibilities and challenges of this with ease. If I had not had this type of training I would never have trusted myself enough or had the confidence to do so. Trust in self allows you to move forward into new things, testing life on all levels with increasing confidence.

Trusting self means that you allow yourself to assess which are the correct decisions for your future, knowing that you can correct the ones that do not work out with confidence. Having trust and responsibility within self helps take a great deal of fear away from any decision-making process in you life. Many people are rendered stagnate in their own lives, immobilised by the fear of change and the decision to do so.

> *Our thoughts like plumbing need unblocking now and then.*

This lack of trust stops people from driving cars, having babies, not going into business or a new relationship. To have trust is to know that if you do not have all the knowledge for what you are about to do, the information will show up in some form or other and you are quite capable of finding it out.

When you trust self you are then in charge of your destiny. You understand your thinking process and are prepared to test it at will.

The very purpose of looking at our emotions and fears is to make you more aware of the mind's processes. Your mind is only a tool and only believes what you tell it. It is the computer and memory of all of the experiences in all the corridors and chambers and dungeons of the castle of your mind. The mind is used in the process of gathering information which it structures into beliefs and opinions and set thoughts which then become habits. Mind becomes our way of perceiving our reality and our own identity. All this makes up the whole self and is projected in our personality and behaviour.

> *Everything you know about self corresponds to a belief you are holding.*

The mind gets stuck on all sorts of memory from experiences, mental, emotional, physical and spiritual. You can change your responses to these once your level of conscious awareness understands which area it is stuck. Our higher consciousness is far greater and has control over our mind. If we wish to change our mind then we need to activate our conscious awareness. The mind can be a tyrant and we can only gain freedom from it by becoming consciously aware of how we think and why we think the way we do. Part of our learning is to see past our own mind games and the limits this places on us. No one person's mind is better than any one else's.

We all have the same size brain and similar molecules and structure which makes up our bodies. We were not meant to be victims in this life. If you think you are then you will be. It is only our difference in experience and thought that separates us at anytime. It is how one chooses to use one's mind that sets us apart from others. Just as it is our intentions upon setting out to perform a deed that gives us away.

> *As you think so shall you be.*
> *Loving thoughts help connect us.*
> *Fearful thoughts only separate us.*

All fearful thoughts separate us and make us feel alone in the world, but all loving thoughts that are shared connect us to all living things. It is so simple to choose a loving thought for self or others over a fearful one. Love has a healing quality and fear has a destructive quality. Only you will see the difference in time once you consciously make better choices with your own thinking.

Difficulties can be overcome and life will seem much better when you grasp the workings of the corridors of the mind. A true master of the mind has the ability upon finding a dungeon within; to immediately look for a way out and solve this knowing that there will be answers for the solution. This is a true warrior, no longer fearful, in search of the self and of the soul.

To be able to climb the castle walls of your mind and roam around within is to know it intimately. This will empower you in your search for self and your soul's purpose.

When you have mastered your mind it will be a most powerful tool. This will be seen within your intentions and the deeds that follow in action. You have the ability to turn any thought into form with the power of the mind. You will finally be able to focus on what is important to your life; finding purpose while understanding just what your priorities are.

Chapter 4
Doorways to the Soul

Through the castle of our mind and the chambers of our heart are the hidden doorways to our soul. The very purpose of the soul is to remind us of who we are, why we are here and what we are here to do. This chapter will help explain the means with which we get in touch with our soul. Exposing the many doorways that soul enters our lives will help you to know where to look.

During my youth I didn't read anything about the soul and didn't understand its purpose or what it really was. As a child I attended Sunday school and was informed that when we died we went to heaven and that our soul moved on. I took this to mean that our soul went to heaven, and confused as I was I accepted this, still not sure what it all meant.

Nobody ever explained the meaning between our soul or spirit. Not having been born to a religious family, I was not lectured in the scriptures of the Bible but knew of Jesus and his disciples and the Ten Commandments.

This to a child from the sixties seemed quite enough for me and I refused to get into any kind of religious debate about the soul or spirit. Instead, I fobbed it all off as myth and legend that had nothing to do with my life. It wasn't until much later I found out more about the soul as I needed to go in search of the answers to my questions about life.

Many people had said to me when I was growing up that I was an 'old soul' and very wise for my age. This all sounded a bit crazy to a sixties teenager fighting to be allowed to go out with boys. What did soul mean and what was an old soul? I had always believed that soul was a place within our bodies and was housed somewhere inside us.

Soul is a strange thing to try and describe to others as we all have our own religious beliefs. But soul is not about religion. Soul, as I know it, is our eternal essence and has our memory past, present and future. It contains all levels of our consciousness including karma, realised self and unrealised self. It is our super computer and the core of our being. It is in total our individuality, who we really are! Man is a soul.

The soul has four main layers surrounding it: physical body, emotional body, mental body and the spiritual body.

Your soul knows who you are, where you've come from, where you are going to and just why you are here. Having discovered this over a period of time and telling you now makes me realise why we seek it out and just how important it is to connect with it.

Soul Music

I remember hearing the phrase, 'that has real soul', but I still didn't understand what was meant by soul. I thought back then that it must have something to do with black American soul music. I loved music, which sometimes gave me goose bumps for reasons I did not understand. I found over the years that many different kinds of music had this affect on me. Old melodies and native drums gave me a deep sense of joy.

> *Soul music*
> *Music through our ears is a message to the soul,*
> *that peace is here for us as every note unfolds.*
> *These melodies transport us to a time so far away.*
> *'Twas in another life that soul heard this music play.*
> *It triggers a remembrance of times in other places*
> *with people you're unable to remember their faces.*
> *The feelings in your heart sends goose bumps everywhere.*
> *Lost loves and melodious tunes reminds us that we cared.*
> *The magic of this music helps our soul stay in touch.*
> *The message we are getting is needed very much.*

Music is one of the doorways to the soul and each time I had heard drums or old melodies it triggered a remembrance from deep within my soul. No wonder we get goose bumps. I have a deep love of Celtic music and it can move me to tears. It gives me a sense of peace and the melancholy memories feed my soul. I am sure that you too have this kind of feeling with certain kinds of music that you love.

The first time I came to understand about soul and its deep inner feelings was through this connection with music. People the world over congregate to listen to all kinds of music that moves the soul, such as opera, classical, African, South American, folk and Celtic, just to name a few. We now have New Age music which has given birth to a whole different sound. It's a blend of all other music and also uses the sounds of nature to soothe the soul and calm our spirit. It is very inspiring listening.

We now know that some healing is carried out using harmonics (sound vibrational noises). The voice is the messenger of the soul, whether it is through the spoken word or through song, it is carried by the voice. So someone's voice can touch the soul in a very special way.

Windows to the Soul

Greetings from our soul can be felt in many ways, but we can feel and know it instantly through the meeting of our eyes. Have you ever looked directly into a stranger's eyes and had the feeling that you have known them before? This is a very common soul remembrance. It is letting you know on another level within your psyche that you have had dealings with this person or their soul in a past life.

This might not always be a pleasant memory. It's possible that you may have had a negative experience with this soul and instantly dislike them for no apparent reason. Or you may feel that your souls are in some way connected and you have work to do in this life together.

A rapport with each other is usually established at this time and you may part company feeling quite happy or unhappy at the meeting and not always really sure why. For some this can be the beginning of trusting their intuition or sixth sense as we call it.

Many people have heard the expression 'windows to the soul' when talking about the eyes. Our external life nowadays is like a continual jungle overgrowing our true soul purpose and our eyes help us distinguish what is relevant to our growth and what is not. The path of self realisation is important to our soul's growth and as we peel away the layers of restrictions created by our external needs and our emotional desires, we see the path of our soul more clearly. We learn to use the eyes to visually discern our truth from non-truth. They become powerful teachers.

It is said that a true visionary can see beyond what is in front of him or her. Given a set of circumstances we should all be able to see what the real meaning and message behind these lessons are. This is why we have eyes to help us see what is beyond and for our soul to recognise its former learning, and also what is needed to learn this time around.

Windows of life

Eyes are the windows of the soul
with which illusions we undress.
The visions they illuminate to us
of the lessons we need to address.
It is no mistake that we cannot see
through another person's eyes.
It's necessary for you to navigate
through your own inherited lies.
The pilgrimage has already been set,
the memory of which you have naught.
These telescopes are to help you view
the things you need to be taught.

Blind people use their other senses as tools for discernment, such as hearing, or touch, or their intuition which is sometimes called the sixth sense. Some have a remarkable sense of smell while others develop a psychic awareness out of need. The same can be said for people who are deaf. They too develop other means of discern-ment. A deaf person can develop an extraordinary perception through touch. Not as you or I would know it. They 'see' by feeling energy through vibrations. Some learn to pick up vibrations through their bodies well before you or I would see what is happening. It just goes to show how the human species has learnt to compensate for any short comings it may have. If one person can learn these things why can't we also? I believe we can all learn to do these things with practice.

Connecting with Nature

Mother Nature opens another doorway for the soul to enter our lives. Nothing can open you up as fast as nature in its magnificence. Viewing a sunset or gazing out at the horizon will help you to connect with your soul.

If ever you need a reminder of the big scheme of things take a trip into a tropical rainforest and feel the nature spirits all around you. I always come back energised when I go for long nature walks.

When you connect with your soul through nature, you want to preserve what little of the natural habitats we have left for the future generations to come, so that they too can feel what you feel. Nature is a big healer as well and it would be sad to see Mother Nature destroyed out of greed.

> **Horizon**
>
> At any given time of day
> we know that it is there,
> where the sky meets the earth
> a place I love to stare.
> I speak of the horizon
> were the clouds all disappear,
> it is colour, it is light,
> it is movement without fear.
> As I sit and ponder deeply
> upon this magic place,
> I feel a sense of joy
> begin to creep across my face.
> For I have seen you many times
> but never are you the same,
> I know not what tomorrow brings
> upon viewing you again.

Most other senses are doorways to the soul. Have you not smelt something only to have it remind you of something else, not just from this life? The smell of horses is a connection with nature that has a deep soul memory for me. When I first laid eyes on a horse in this life I knew that I could ride. Even now the mere smell of horses or stables brings back memories so ancient for me.

I had a pony when I was growing up. Many of my most fondest memories are of galloping along with friends trying to keep up. It made me feel free and fearless when I was on my pony's back. It helped me see the world around me from a different perspective. My horse helped rescue me from despair many times.

Oh Noble Horse

Over cobbled streets and fields of grass
and mountain tracks we rode.
Through pebbled streams and sandy shores
and crops of wheat you strode.
My memories of you noble horse
reach back into the past.
As trusty steed both strong and brave
who's heart was there to last.
With nostrils flared and ears alert
and long tail flexed up high.
'Twas nature at its bold and best
as you rode across the sky.

Throughout the centuries of our time
man has known no better friend.
They were with us through our bitter wars
loyal companions to the end.
We trusted him and we harnessed him
his spirit we tried to break.
Instead we learned to honour his grit
for his spirit we could never take.
I tell you that this noble horse
has been there for us all.
He who is eager to ride his back
will feel that noble call.

I was a loner and a warrior when I was with my horse. Many people connect with nature through pets and animals. It is the very reason we see more people becoming vegetarians. The movie 'Babe' had much to do with children giving up eating bacon and other pork products after viewing the film. Connecting with the soul and feeling the spirit of an animal can be very rewarding indeed.

For many of us the love of an animal has been a catalyst and a beginning of an opening for a doorway to the soul. The love of an animals spirit connects us with our soul opening our heart. This doorway through the heart is the biggest doorway for the soul to enter our lives. The heart is where we are taught the many lessons about love and also where love of self must enter. It is in knowing the self and loving the self that connects us and establishes a bigger picture of real unconditional love.

Love, it seems, is the vehicle used most for personal growth, directly connecting us with our soul. It en-compasses all of our intellect, our emotions and our physical being as well as connecting to our spirit. The heart and soul are linked in holy matrimony and love is the main agenda. Love can be, it seems, one of the biggest reasons we start to soul search in the first place. Usually because of the lack of love in one's life or the many unhappy love affairs some seem to have. These love relationships we have, however, help to teach us valuable lessons about self and about love.

It is through the mirroring we receive in our relationships and our interaction with others that become big teachers of self, especially our emotional self.

As the heart opens it experiences love of various kinds and allows more soul to be displayed in our lives. The communication between the heart and soul allows us to look at our honesty and honour of self and others. It is this integrity that develops better love relationships.

It allows us to take responsibility for the love we receive as well as give. The depth of love one receives as well as gives is also an indication of being in touch with one's soul.

We begin to understand that there are many different kinds of love. The kind of love we give to a child is usually unconditional love, and no matter what that child does or says you always come back to love it. Mind you, we don't always like them and the things they do, however, we always love them. This is true paternal love, or unconditional love.

It is up to us to find out about the many different types of love in our life, and to discern which is correct and which is not. Lust is not love, and sex can only be a physical expression of love if love really exists between the consenting adults.

It is enough to say that it is in the seeking of love that we begin to learn about it. Eventually you are led in a circle back to self love, discovering that unless you learn to love yourself completely, then it is impossible to expect someone else to love all of you.

This is why the heart is an important doorway for the soul, as it is through the heart we feel all of our love emotions. However, they are read and interpreted by the mind. In other words they are intellectualised through our reflected beliefs, usually about self. So, if you have any self doubts they are usually reflected within your love relationships.

Love of self is a hard lesson but self realisation leads to many other discoveries about who we are and why we are here, all in search of souls purpose.

I was one of the many who always sought to find the one true love, the perfect man, my mate for life, the one who would match me on all levels. People thought I was crazy, but I believed in this so strongly that nothing would let me think that this did not exist. Through many trial and error types of relationships and different kinds of loves and even a bad marriage, I was searching for the one love of all, my soulmate. It wasn't until I learnt to love myself that I was ready to meet him, and yes he finally arrived out of the blue.

When you stop searching and allow the natural course of events to take place then you attract things that are meant to happen. My soul and his soul were meant to be together in this life and we have work to do also as twin flames. When or if this is meant to happen to you, you will have a knowing about it.

Soul Knows

As we met our souls rejoiced
for this was finally the right choice.
It was our destiny for us to meet
through our eyes the souls did greet.
'Twas already known and understood
that we're together for the highest good.
To help evolve the human race
and make the world a better place.

Although we did not understand
love had already been planned.
We haven't ever had a doubt
of what this love would be about.
Our souls decided to let us know
we both came from the same glow.
The light it shone from our love
to serve a purpose from above.

Good loves are there for all of us if we look in the right places, especially if you love yourself enough to wait. I believe there is someone special for everybody. It is the impatience of wanting love that makes people seek the wrong kinds of partners and settle for a less than perfect love. Some people seek a different kind of love like Mother Teresa whose love of humanity was enormous. Lots of love in love relationships pales in existence compared to this kind of selfless love.

There are more doorways to the soul and some of these are small but relevant, such as the written word in books and poetry. When something hits a cord deep within you then recognise this as talking to your soul. The more you tune into these kinds of intuitive messages, the more strength you give to your existence and to the soul. There can be no stronger feeling than the direct validation from the soul, keeping you in touch with self.

Our intuition is another big doorway for the soul. We quite often get hunches about certain things through dreams and gut feelings. These hunches come through to us as intuitive thoughts and are received as messages from the soul.

Intuition is the intelligence of the soul's higher self. It lets you feel what is true within your mind's eye rather than know what is true with your mind only. Your intuition opens you up to the unknowable, to what is unfamiliar to you. This helps the energy of what you need to experience to flow directly to you. The soul is unafraid of the unknowable and we are all pilgrims on the pathway to the unknown.

Doubt destroys our intuition and sabotages the messages we are meant to receive. That is why I spoke of the over-growing jungle of everyday life. This intrusive jungle comes in many forms, but mainly it is the complex mental environment with which we now live. Our minds are intruded upon by the many new belief systems, all the commercial messages, and lets not forget the news stories and sensationalism and hype from the press.

New health warnings and technological gadgetry, along with an explosion of entertainment options, are all vying for our attention. The disturbing thing about this issue is that all the noise and messages we are distracted by are only other people finding their own way, on their path back to self in search of soul.

The regular peeling away of this debris is part of the stress of everyday life. We need to become more aware of this to be able to overcome the difficulties of staying in touch with self, while staying open to our own messages from soul.

Learning not to get distracted by the many options whilst staying open to new experience can seem a little daunting at first, but if you can keep your main goals in mind this will help keep you on track. You will find your power always in balance between mind and intuition.

During the course of our lives we receive information from all levels of mind, body and spirit. Understanding which part of you is talking to you comes from the desire to make better decisions based on self love and intuitive feelings.

The soul is like a computer of our past, present and future. It has the capability to remember what it has learnt from this life thus far and other lifetimes. The purpose of this soul memory is to bring forth valuable information when needed. When you begin to tap into your very being and listen to the call of your soul, you will discover the depth of your memory and inner knowing. Some things that you have had no conscious memory or knowledge of will start to enter your life. Accessing the soul's memory is very powerful.

When we consciously open doorways to the soul we start to evaluate ourselves in depth. Trying to be honest about all aspect of our nature. We begin to look at our positive and negative self. Needing to integrate both of these on all levels, physically, mentally, emotionally and spiritually. This is an awakening time for all that you now know about self, especially the negatives.

It is this integration of the negative self that opens up another doorway to the soul. True power lies in individuality and the ability to see yourself through your own eyes and not through the eyes of another. We now understand that we wish to feed the soul and its purpose, and so we must look for a way to earn a living that is totally compatible with our soul.

When you think of yourself as separate from your soul, you obstruct the current and your own power will defeat you. Learn to identify the form of personal power you need, what you want to accomplish with it, or build with it, or create with it, and become that. Then there will be no separation from your soul self.

> *Work should be love made visible.*

Many people during this time find that they need to change jobs for their purpose to be fulfilled. It is the very reason people drop out of mainstream society and look for a better existence and more meaning to life. When we evolve our consciousness to this stage we become vehicles for change, not only with self but the community and the globe. Change is another doorway to the soul. Every time you decide on some form of change you invite the soul to enter.

Those of you who are afraid of change are not quite in touch with your soul. Because of this you may find it hard to trust life to be there for you, seeking to control it by staying in your comfort zones. People who dislike change are afraid of the future. Another fear-born event coming from ego.

When you are in touch with your soul all life becomes important as you now see a much bigger picture. The soul knows the many truths within our lives and seeks to expose them, helping to enlighten us into our own knowing and truer selves. When the doorways to our soul are flung open there is no need to fear and turn back. Aligned with our soul we move forward with purpose.

Life takes on a whole new existence.

Chapter 5
Upon Love the Soul Walks

Love has been talked about, sung about, danced about and written about. It is the most widely used vehicle for conversations of various types and helps to advertise more products than we can begin to speak of. Love it seems is in great demand the world over. So where does it begin, how do we find it, and why do we need love?

Initially, as our soul is given the right to passage and we arrive on the planet, we come to understand that love comes from the lovely lady called our mother. She nurtures us, suckles us and takes care of all our needs in the beginning of our life. We feel a deep sense of connection to her as she comforts and loves us. We then discover that she has a mate and he is our father. He helps to give us love and nurture us also, but it is not the same kind of connection as our mother's. We experience two types of love energy from our parents, the female and male.

Some of us have sisters and brothers born into this family as well, and we experience some love and nurturing from them also and their love is a different kind of love. Of course, there are children who, for some reason, do not experience love in this fashion at all. They may have been orphaned or abandoned, but usually there is some form of love given to help nurture a newborn baby.

Whatever our experience is, this is where we fashion our first understanding about love. It is a simple understanding of comfort and security, safety and warmth. This first kind of love gives us strength as it helps us to feel that we are perfect and accepted by our family for who we are. There are no expectations placed on a newborn baby.

We begin to believe love is always going to be there from our parents and family. Usually it does remain. However, it can change as we grow up and develop with our needs and the expectations of others. Our first inklings and feelings of love, as we know it, are of the unconditional kind, especially from our mother.

It is this unconditional kind of love we seek to find in the rest of our world.

As children we play and grow, learn about friends, life and love. It all seems fairly uncomplicated.

In these early years we are learning about our environment and how we fit in. If we have pets we feel great affection for them as we do for our friends also. This is all part of love. It is innocent love of the purest kind, usually made without judgement. Young children do not know how not to love everyone. They have no need to discriminate with their love at this stage.

Then one day we begin slowly to change within our own body and mind. The beginnings of sexuality rears its head. Not understanding this we are confused. Hopefully, we have had wonderful parents who explained about puberty, what it was and how it would now effect our whole life for the better. For some this is an amazing time of self discovery and for others it is a fearful time, full of confusion, ridicule and disappointments.

Sex verses Love

Luckily, this phase doesn't take too long, but what we experience about love during this period of growing up can effect our lives for some time to come. Love and the opposite sex can become issues during this time as does one's own sexual desires. Our body and our brain, it seems, get together to conspire and taunt us. Our emotions run rampant as new hormones are released into our system. We begin to come to terms with the fact that life will never be the same again and childhood is leaving us forever. This can be a very strange time.

Love takes on a whole new meaning. Because of our confused state of being we seek love and validation. Not from our parents any more because we think that they don't know what it is like to be us and a teenager, but from each other. As we struggle to fit into a new world, leaving behind us the freedom of our childhood innocence, we feel vulnerable and awkward.

We notice the changes within our own bodies, so it is only natural that we notice each other's bodies changing as well. We see that girls develop breasts and curves that drive boys crazy when flaunted. We notice the boys developing muscles and hairy bodies. Their voice changes and there's a bulge which develops in their groin quite often. Boys talk to each other about sex, cars and sport, while girls talk about romantic love, fashion, boys and make-up.

Boys and girls, for a short time, forget about the unconditional love they use to receive from home. They experiment with each other with physical and emotional behaviour in search for recognition.

Strange things begin to happen to your psyche and a friend of the opposite sex that you may have had now becomes the object of your new sexual attraction. Not sure why you have these thoughts but still seeking their friendship it all gets too much. You begin communicating in new ways with touching and flirting with your eyes, sending messages to each other's brains. Before you know it you are both kissing and cuddling and this feels exciting.

This is where girls, especially, think that it is love they are experiencing and not just sexual desire. The boys, however, experience a different sensation, usually in their groin in the form of an erection. They experience sexual desire and not necessarily love of any sort. An emotional and physical cocktail develops within the mind and body. Both sexes fantasise about would-be events in this new found pleasure.

> *Lust is nature's way of convincing you that you are in love.*

It becomes apparent to boys that to experience the sexual act they must relay to the girl that they love her. Boys are much too excited about the prospect of sex to worry about the trivia's of love. Girls are much too excited about love to be worried about the trivialities of boys' sexual desires. Both learn to give one to receive the other.

Boys use love for sex and girls use sex for love in these early adolescent years. They embark on a sexual career that leads to all sorts of life's dramas and new mysteries. When growing into young men and women we begin to understand the principles of lust; its highs and its lows, its trauma and fun, all of which we are in a hurry to experience. How innocent we were in the beginning, finding out about sexual desires fueled with passion and feelings of love.

Lust, it seems, has played its part as a catalyst for the relationships between man and woman for their continued learning about love. Yet to fully understand our own sexuality we keep experimenting with lust until we understand its principals and the responsibilities.

Through lust we learn about our gender and what it has to teach us about our role in society. While experimenting with lust, we learn about ourselves and how we effect each other in our sexual relationships. It is through our relationships that we come to understand more fully our emotions and the part they play in our life. Falling in and out of love over and over seems to be a favourite pastime of the young and those who are still searching for real love whilst finding out about themselves.

> ### The Principles of lust
>
> Man has the power, woman has the need
> to be his receptor and accept his seed.
> The power of love and the depth of desire
> have been man's quest through lust we aspire,
> to quench the yearning we see in our eyes,
> for love the burning manifests in our thighs.
> When man begets woman and enters her need
> he's then confronted with his eternal greed.
> To own and conquer this woman in sight
> 'tis the animal in man, his lust in full flight.
> For woman 'tis love she seeks through her thighs,
> she chooses to see past his animal lies.
>
> Surrendering her being to her man with trust
> that what he seeks with her is not his own lust.
> Man learns about love through the body he drives
> deep into this woman he loves and now thrives.
> When man is presented with love from a child
> that he's co-created with his woman mild.
> An amazing thing happens to him you will see
> for his lust takes on another reality.
> This responsibility has now changed their life,
> his lust takes form in love of family and wife.
> 'Twas the sharing of love that helped lend a hand,
> through lust they have learnt about life and man.

Looking for Intimacy

Love is the strongest energy we have, and it is by the giving and receiving of love that we grow spiritually. It is through the opening of the heart that we experience the feelings of love, and where our thoughts of true love are greeted by our soul. These are the main reasons we ardently seek a partner - to give and receive love. The pairing up of our society has been going on for centuries for this very reason.

Men and woman are different, not only in their physical bodies but also within their emotions and how they express them, especially in a relationship. Their mental attitudes towards each other and the world at large differ also.

Men and women experience love differently, and depending on their childhood experiences, they either show affection and love openly, or they have trouble expressing their real feelings toward the opposite sex.

It is the need for love that helps men and women learn how to give love in its true context and in an appropriate manner. There is no crime in loving too much, only in the lack of it. This is felt very strongly within relationships where one partner is more loving than another. For a time we may choose to try to change the other partner, always seeking ideas to coerce them into showing their love. Alas, this is not a good idea. Seeking another's love is the big mistake. Love can only be given, not taken by force or persuasion.

It is when we feel alone and lonely that the need for love becomes amplified. So often we settle for a less than perfect relationship out of need, and this seems to be a simple solution to our loneliness for a time. Possibly, we have experienced this before and have been hurt emotionally in some way, but eventually the need for comfort and love is too great. When we have healed from this, feeling emotionally stronger and still needing to be nurtured, we seek love out again.

> *Loneliness is a call from your soul for love of self.*

Somehow lust loses its shine along the way and we accept that we do have physical desires and needs. However, these only play one part in the total experience of the love we're seeking.

Dissatisfied with love we begin to look at other areas in our life for fulfillment such as our career and business, or with sport, the arts and hobbies and friends. Men, for a time, can get caught up in this area as it distracts them. Many men have trouble opening up to women about their feelings, especially if they have been hurt in a relationship.

Life becomes a little empty if we are left to pursue our work and ambitions only. Eventually, we realise that we are alone in our life's pursuits. The lack of love starts us wanting to share all this with a partner. We now wish to have more than just physical interaction with a partner when we recognise that sex, while it can be great and satisfying on one level, is not really love.

When we understand something is missing in our lives, even with these kinds of fulfilling interests, we still need to seek love. By taking time to look for a companion instead of a beautiful lust partner, we seek someone that has similar interests of mind. We have progressed beyond only the physical desires and we seek more mental and emotional ones.

We need to learn to share more of ourselves with a new partner. Learning to exchange feelings through the sharing of conversation whilst trying not to feel silly or vulnerable is difficult in the beginning. This is sharing of a different kind and can be quite scary at first.

This is the beginning of true intimacy. Intimacy is when you are invited to tell someone who you are on the inside and then they do the same. To be open to receive love one must be vulnerable by being open and unafraid of sharing our inner selves; to expose to another human being our feelings about all kinds of things.

When a man and a woman get together and show real feelings for one another, sharing their most intimate thoughts without holding back, including silly fears and phobias, it is then that they feel safe, loved, understood and cared about. The trust that develops between them bonds them together in a deeper understanding of each other and real unconditional love can develop. It is this level of sharing that makes for good marriages.

When a child is created through love it then serves to remind the young parents who have co-created it about their first knowing of love, the unconditional kind from their own mother. There is nothing like paternal love to remind us of real unconditional love.

A new understanding of love is reborn and a new soul is created. For most parents, giving birth to a child has the effect also of giving birth to a new love consciousness and a new awareness about responsibility and commitment to loving the child and each other.

For most women giving birth, this gives love a whole new potential. A doorway opens and our soul greets us yet again through our heart. It is impossible not to love the innocence of a newborn child. We settle into the unconditional nurturing and caring of this new life that we have created, learning all over again about the giving and receiving of love.

Love's Expectations

For some couples, children do not come along until much later, and so they learn about love through other means. They have more time to explore their world and test themselves in careers and the like, finding out about the different types of love in relationships along the way.

> *For love it is eternal,*
> *It matters not whence it came.*
> *Who cares where it lands,*
> *So long as it remains.*

We never forget the feeling when we experience love. It fills us up and floods over into the rest of our life, effecting everyone around us. The feeling of love is contagious. Can you remember being around someone in love? How crazy they become, how they forget things and drift off into another heads pace with a smile a mile wide on their face. What could be more pleasing than to feel like that most of the time? Could love remain forever?

The stumbling block for us all in our love relationships is the expectations we place on the people we love. It seems that once we have found someone to love and settle into a solid relationship with, we seek to make them to our likeness, or try to. A big mistake!

We must remember what it was that we loved in the first place and seek not to change what was perfect already. Accepting the differences between the sexes are where real grown-ups survive. Understanding that we all have a soul and that it is different to our own is very important. We should never seek to own another's love for it is given only through free will.

> *It is when we place demands*
> *on the love given that*
> *we begin to destroy it.*

Sadly, this happens quite often for some. They blame their partners, parents and friends for the lacking which they crave, not realising that they are creating the problems through their own expectations.

For many of us the journey to love takes a long time and we make many mistakes along the way while we are learning.

As a young girl I felt that love should be deep, strong and special or sacred. I was guilty of being one of those girls who tried to turn a weekend of lust into a lifetime of love. I had many disappointments along the way with a very unhappy first marriage from which I had two beautiful daughters.

Learning to understand myself led to my understanding why it was necessary for me to go through all the pains of failed love relationships. I had to find out what didn't work to find out what did eventually. Throughout all my traumas I never gave up on love. Sure, for a while I was a little cynical about love and men but deep within I still believed that there was a true love for me somewhere; so I bravely journeyed on.

Love's Journey

I've traveled some distance,
my journey has been long.
I know you're out there waiting,
I'll continue to be strong.
You are my destiny my love,
the power behind my drive.
And in my hours of weakness
your vision kept me alive.
There have been many tests
of strength along this love's trail,
but my belief of one true love
would never let me fail.
I am a noble princess
your lover and your friend.
I will journey far to find you
to be together in the end.

After my divorce I spent many years alone as a single woman having vowed never to marry again. It was during this time that I learned a great deal about myself and of love and life. Raising my two daughters gave me many challenges that helped with growth physically, mentally, emotionally and spiritually.

I was to learn through many relationships just what I did and didn't want from love and my partner. Mostly, I learnt about myself, how I reacted to love and the men that tried to love me. I came to understand about conditional love, placing conditions on the amount of love given, usually because of expectations. I learnt about co-dependant relationships, emotionally needing someone more than they wanted or needed me and leaning on them for my every support.

I soon realised that these types of love relationships no longer appealed to me as being ideal. I found myself loving men who for some reason were not available to me in some way. Some were available mentally and physically and we matched, but we clashed emotionally and spiritually or we just didn't meet on those levels. Some were matched on three levels - mental, emotional and spiritual but not physical. When I began to notice this I made a measuring scale and compared some of my more serious relationships, asking myself some honest questions about which areas we were matched. Sounds corny but it all served to make me look at what my relationships consisted of.

This gave me an idea of how my choices of partners rated and made it very clear to me what was missing. A match with a partner on all levels of mind, body and spirit was important for me. No longer was I prepared to settle for anything less than this. You may think that this is impossible to have, but it is not. I began sharing this feeling with some of my male friends, only to be told that there is no such thing as the perfect match. Having made the decision to have a match on all these levels, I proceeded to make what I called my 'wish list of qualities' that my dream man would need to have.

Now I can hear you saying this woman must have been mad. No, just getting real and specific about my needs, wants and desires. If you don't know what you want, the universe cannot deliver it to you when you're ready. And so it was that I got specific about this and many other areas of my life.

I had always been goal orientated for many years, having been involved with sales training and staff motivation. So it didn't take me long to work it out that if I didn't have a goal in this area it was never going to happen.

Faith in Love

We create our own destiny and must take the responsibility of this seriously if we wish to achieve a specific end result. It took some time for me to create this list of qualities and as newer things came to mind I would write them down. By just creating this list of my perfect man's qualities, it was an affirmation that I believed he actually existed. It had the effect of hope and opened me up to possibilities in all directions.

My cynicism died and my faith in love returned. No longer was I the cynical divorcee; instead I became a born-again romantic. I tried not to let my head rule my heart completely anymore. I opened up to receive love no matter where it came. I stopped thinking about love and allowed for it to enter my life on its own. I believed it would happen when the time was right and that was enough. I even told people that my soulmate was on his way. Of course, we just laughed at that, but still I would believe. I got on with my life of business and the raising of my children while I waited for him to turn up.

I read many books about relationships during this time. I found some very interesting things about men and myself and highly recommend them to you. One was He Says, She Says: Closing the Communication Gap Between the Sexes by Lillian Glass, and the other was, Men are from Mars and Women are from Venus, by John Gray. These were so full of the events that had taken place in so many of my relationships, I thought they must have known me personally. I was to discover some of my relationship patterns and dramas that I helped co-create.

They went something like this:
- Loving only the potential in a man instead of who he was now or wished to be in the future.
- Always waiting and wanting them to be something they were not.
- Blaming their shortcomings instead of looking at my wants.
- Seeing how I always wanted to be right and how I placed myself in competition with the opposite sex.

I realised that through all my relationships I was trying to be validated but never succeeded, and so I spent most of my time seeking their approval. This was a leftover, emotional drama from my childhood which had to do with my father. I was never validated by him, nor did he give me any kind of recognition. Dad wasn't into praise and even to this day never says 'well done' for any achievement. I also realised that I was giving my love conditionally in the hope that all would be appreciated and then reciprocated.

This meant I was seeking love outside of myself from others, instead of looking at myself and learning to love myself first. It was to be a huge learning curve for me, as I had grown up in a very male-dominated house with four brothers and a strong, intimidating father. I prided myself on knowing about the opposite sex and under-standing them, which was true to a degree. However, I was to see this theory shot to pieces as I discovered my many misgivings about me, love and relationships.

> *It was I that was the fraud lacking real self love.*

Understanding the many facets of love is part of the soul's evolvement. We, as a people, seem to believe that love is an external experience. We seek love from others in a physical or emotional form, to provide our self worth and validate our identity. In doing this we are living by the needs of our outer egos personalities rather than our true inner heart's desires. Eventually we tire of this kind of co-dependant love as it falls short of our expectations. It was too hard to sustain. I was confused and dissatisfied for a while, and unable to understand why. I became aware that strong emotional love was a dependant kind of love and could be a burden and a trap if it was repeated constantly.

Looking for love is stating that you wish to learn to love self. The need to find that unconditional love of self means connecting with your soul. We seem to focus instead on the things we believe that love lacks and look to improve on it. We only confirm the belief that love is something external that we must acquire it to have self worth. We get hung up on our external needs and lose the real meaning of love.

Our emotions and our ego lead us astray and before you know it you find yourself divorced with a couple of children wondering what happened and where did it go wrong. It is in the searching for your true self that you delve into these emotional battles, exposing your dramas for what they are.

It is our soul that saves the day by leading us through a maze of experiences to help us see just what love really is. We seek love first from our parents. From them we learn our first understandings about what love is and how it is displayed. Our parents also let us look at the female and male roles. We base a lot of our early learning on how we perceive these roles to be. I have found that many of us need to seek out our truths about love before we can begin to understand our parents and the way they gave of their love; not only to each other but to us as their children.

Communicating about Love

Love is the very reason we need to be with each other. It is the one common denominator that connects us all. We all seek love because we want to feel connected, but the real love connection we're seeking is with self. We believe that to be connected we must seek love, and love for some this equals touch and therefore sex. Again, seeking affirmation that the external world of our physical being is where love is found.

During a sexual experience many couples get in touch with their soul because they are sharing a very intimate experience with another person. This validates part of their being.

When in a truly loving relationship, the sexual side helps couples explore the depth of their feelings towards each other. They mirror their mental, emotional, physical and spiritual beliefs of what love really is. No wonder we seek validation and approval this way. It also helps to explain why some people are afraid of sex and intimacy; they are extremely confronting.

If you experience self doubts it will be expressed in your love relationships. This helps to explain why many people seek love via sexual encounters.

> *What prevents you from getting the love you want?*

Learning while waiting became my pastime and I enjoyed it very much. It's strange but I actually stopped feeling lonely somewhere along the way. My focus had obviously shifted, which allowed me to move on within my own consciousness. I still met and had the odd male companion, who all became good friends, and we shared a great deal as we talked openly about love and relationships.

This was new for me as most men weren't interested in talking unless it meant sex afterwards. However, I found that these new men were in the same boat as many women. They were waiting for that special person to love and to be loved in return. They had found, like me, that communicating was a far superior way of getting to know someone.

While men and women are different, their individual needs and desires were basically the same, only they manifest in different forms. I found some very sensitive men out there who were all tired of being used by women, just as some women are tired of being used by men.

It became obvious to me through communication that I was being mirrored by these men who were also needing to find themselves and connect with love. They were looking for their 'soulmate'.

What I was to discover from them became important. I was accepting that men could be equal to me. I could feel connected to them without feeling any pressure for a sexual relationship or the 'falling in love, lost in love' kind of relationship. I also stopped feeling the need to be in competition with the male species. We could actually be best friends and share very intimate thoughts and feelings without the attachment of a relationship. I enjoyed this very much as I know they did also, and we all grew as a result of this. We talked about the perfect mates and shared male and female points of view, especially about communication in most areas of a love relationship; and we talked openly about sex.

Soulmates

The most stimulating of the conversations revolved around the concept of a soulmate (the perfect mate).

As a concept of deeper love, I was fascinated by it. I needed to know more about this as I had always had a deep yearning to find my perfect mate. Finally, I was to discover why this was so important to me.

My higher self and soul realised that we were all once connected on a soul level at one time. The source from whence we came must have decided to experience all manner of things. To do so it would be necessary to divide soul groups into smaller parts or groups. These groups were then divided into smaller soul families (soulmates), and then into individual souls, which sometimes split into two, creating twin souls.

These twin souls were created so that they could experience being separate, lonely and isolated through many incarnations. It is said that they were put to task and their deepest need to be together was tested over many life times. This is why we have the saying, 'If you love someone set them free, if they come back to you then the love is true.'

> **Upon Love the Soul Walks**
>
> Would that you feel my love for you
> deep within your soul.
> And with our bodies loved coiled embrace
> we stare deeply into self.
> And into the mouth of love we walk unashamed,
> only to feel the passion of its breath
> fill our being and carry us away.
> For us it can be scary, this our cavern of love,
> yet when deep inside each other
> our love it knows no boundaries.
> It is an expression of our oneness,
> of our own divinity.
> So upon entering this place
> deep within our souls,
> we are reminded of our eternity,
> so that we may die and go to heaven.
> To both be born again,
> in love forever
> with each other's soul.

These unions were stressed and tested which enabled them to work through the many blocks and lessons put before them, helping to evolve their soul.

The soulmate relationship is a very rewarding one and has many profound experiences involving much endurance, integrity and discipline. This couple knows that to stay together they must remain centred in their love for each other. This is one of the reasons it is unique. The many tests they have endured so that they can be together stand them tall in the relationship stakes. They are matched on all levels: the mind, body and spirit. They stand out from the rest because they are a unit and their minds work as one. They tend to intuit each other most of the time and feel what the other is feeling. They
respect each other's uniqueness as individuals but share in their individuality.

When you meet like-minded friends, it is possible they are soulmates or fragments of the original soul group. You will have a deep awareness of this kind of connection because it will have a profound effect upon you. You will feel, by the etheric layer in your aura, other members of your soul family. Spiritually, you will feel at peace and be aware of this well before you are conscious of it. It seems, at the moment, that many soul groups are gathering around the world and bonding together, for the need is great. What was once separate must come together again and be whole. So it is with soulmates, they need to rejoin as do twin souls. Like attracts like so those souls who are vibrating at the same rate will be drawn together. These are special relationships because when they merge as one in marriage their love resonates as the purest kind and is felt by many. It helps strike harmony throughout the entire universe.

> When you unconditionally love someone you are connecting with their very soul.

The sexual union between soulmates or a couple who unconditionally love each other helps to open them up emotionally, mentally and spiritually, to themselves as well as each other.

The very act of lovemaking is a portal to discovering our true selves and orgasm is a glimpse of the bliss felt in eternal life. It is this total state of bliss we seek to experience from puberty on. It is no wonder we had the sexual revelations through the ages of man.

Mass orgies in ancient Roman times were used to experience the bliss of our flesh and orgasm, but I doubt that they knew why they were experiencing this on a spiritual level. To experience orgasm on its own without love feels only physically gratifying, but loses something on all other levels. Women have known this for a long time but it has taken men longer to work this out.

When men and women come together out of real love (the unconditional kind) and unite making love, then they experience the most wondrous emotional deep love connection. It is sad that sometimes this truly beautiful act, intended to remind us of our original being, is exploited, abused and used to pressure men and women both.

To have this total connection we also need to have both polarities, male and female, aligned within oneself. To be in touch with your male and female sides of your nature is to understand the whole of your self, masculine and feminine. Spiritually we have no sex or gender. It is a physical manifestation of the human race and animals alike.

What I came to understand during this time was that women were created to accept and receive men, to nurture and to give birth and to regenerate the human race.

Men were created to give life to their women, to protect and help take care of them and see their children fit for their adult life. It seems man has had to keep learning about love and to connect with his woman regularly to remind him of his priorities.

Love is a priority

It is important that we all learn to love self first, then family and finally others in our community. Man was not made to kill each other for the possession of land or over religious differences.

You will notice that it is not women who go out and kill children and loved ones. This is not how women settle arguments. When there are problems, women look within themselves for the right answers. Women communicate their feelings with the hope of resolving conflict. If a woman has many children to feed and care for, she does not favour one over the other. Instead, she shares and divides evenly what she has amongst her family, and can usually stretch it to feed more if need be. This is how the female energy deals with crisis. She goes within for answers and seeks to serve everybody's interests with love. The male energy looks externally for answers through action of some kind, wanting to control any crisis, usually by force and fueled with anger. Mostly, he is unaware of the consequences to others through his controlling actions.

Man has needed the sexual union with his woman to soften his warrior ways and help him to connect with his own love, enabling him to see this reflected everywhere. So the sexual act, which was for men, originally a lusting physical release, now becomes a means of connecting to his own love through the love he experiences from his woman.

His love and compassion grows and extends out into his community and he helps by showing other men by his deeds of love, compassion and caring. A woman learns to respect and honour her man and this is then reflected to others when the man loves and respects his woman.

We all learn to grow with our knowledge of self as we move through our life's experiences of love and sex. Eventually we come to accept whom we are in total, and open up to a total connection with love and sex with a partner who matches us more fully.

No wonder we all seek to fall in love. It is through love that we all connect with our soul. When our hearts are full of love the world seems brighter and things that would normally bother us don't seem so important. Our love spills out and overflows into everything around us.

The heart has opened to connect with love on this level. This gives us compassion when we are feeling true unconditional love for everyone else and everything else, including our community, environment and planet.

When we connect at this level we are healing not only ourselves but everything around us. All the great masters have been trying to deliver this message for eons, telling us that the path of love is one of the greatest spiritual teachers and a path of true enlightenment. You will find one of the greatest rewards of love is LOVE.

> **Love**
>
> Love is the place in my heart and soul
> where I release the need to have control.
> Love is the person I try reflecting to others,
> sharing and caring for my sisters and brothers.
> Love is the acceptance of everyone I see,
> without judgement I honour and let them be.
> Love is in each breath I breathe each day.
> This miracle of life that supports my stay.
> Love is the sunrise, sunset and morning dew
> and the knowledge all is perfect, yes even you.
> Love is timeless, ageless and always near,
> all I need do is reach out without fear.

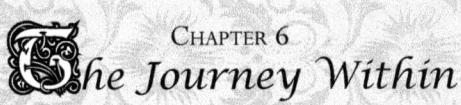

Chapter 6
The Journey Within

As we begin to come to terms with the many aspects of the self, we have begun the journey within to a deeper level of consciousness. Our desire is to understand and integrate what we now know, the way we function mind, body and spirit. It is at this level we connect with our soul's consciousness and learn to deal in only our truths, balancing the good and bad sides of our nature and personality.

The journey of the soul takes a long time. The soul chooses what is necessary for its spirit's growth in this life. Eventually, throughout many lives you would have been many things and everything. The soul remembers the beginning of creation and why it was sent here. Were you not sent here to evolve and grow?

For this to take place did you not have to experience all living things, including the planet, animal, mineral, and vegetable? Are we not the next step in evolvement out of the physicality of matter and into the mental, emotional bodies and eventually back to the spiritual self? Isn't this the very reason we eventually begin the pilgrimage back to our soul, looking through all the debris in our life, sifting out what matters to us and what doesn't, helping us to sort out just what our real priorities are?

After you have done this and know the self in all its entirety, your heart begins its eternal quest inward and connects to the soul and to the spirit. This is called the journey within. For each of us this is a special time because once you pass a certain level of knowledge of self, you will always have that knowledge; there is no turning back. We continually move forward and that means change is inevitable.

This journey takes aeons of time. This is why we need to incarnate through many lifetimes so that we can experience the physicality of matter and human emotion and all there is and complete the mission. It is important for us to be everything and to understand and grow in our knowledge and consciousness so the wisdom we receive in doing so can then be used in new lives in our future and for a higher purpose.

By higher purpose I mean that we will help humanity in some way. I don't mean that we all become saints but we are all teachers in our own right as we learn from each other. Some will be healers and others will work with animals while others help technology and so on. We are all here to serve a purpose and we all evolve into that purpose in our own time frame.

The one thing we all have in common on our journey is the right to our free will and to choose our own experiences. Our choices improve as our awareness grows and the fears we once harboured give way to an open and inquiring mind. Our soul knows what is expected of us and this is what helps to keep us on track. As we journey within we start to look at a much bigger picture, not only of self but of the world at large, as our conscious awareness is linking up with the universe. Realising we are all connected, we notice how we effect others and that we are all affected by each other.

> *We see all of our self in the world and see how we have evolved as a people.*

Our global consciousness (the total of humanity's awareness of life as we know it) has changed as we have evolved through the ages. The journey within makes us look at our religious beliefs also, their origin and how these have effected the world and its people on the journey. It seems to me that man has sought comfort within his spiritual beliefs in the external world also. Man's emotional need for validation, love and recognition has also permeated his spiritual beliefs.

This need for emotional comfort has seen his religious beliefs bend and twist to suit different mindsets and cultures the world over, depending on who you talk to as to whose theories are correct. I have had many a religious fanatic thrust his beliefs at me and challenge me to spiritual combat of a verbal kind.

We have used gods and religious ritual to control people with the fear of not being validated or allowed to enter heaven if we did not believe in a particular religious dogma; or that some evil force would take us to hell if we did not conform to this kind of control belief.

We may have climbed out of the technological Dark Age but it still exists in much of our religions today. The biggest spiritual struggle has been with the different types of organised religious beliefs, verses the path of self realisation. This is not common knowledge but it should be because it is simple in its context.

It is we humans that complicate things with our minds.

The understanding that I have of these differences is that with organised religions you must believe in some form of external patriarchal god or person to find salvation and validation. You must read the *Holy Bible* of your faith's interpretation and live life via a set of rules created by the religious leaders of that time. Whereas with self-realisation you journey within and are 'giving birth' to your own conscious higher self through self awareness. Self spiritualisation is the result of giving birth to one's conscious spirit realisation and coming to terms with one's own spirit or god within (or spirituality) without the dogma of religion or doctrines of any kind. Neither one is right nor wrong. However you wish to perceive your life is up to you.

Crisis of Belief

This spiritual journey comes to us all in many forms. Of course, some do find their way through the many religions as well, but there are many who find their way without them. Whatever your path is in life you must travel it for yourself. During the journey within, many find they experience what is called a crisis of their particular faith, depending on what they believe in. This can happen in many ways; the first is from a material or physical plane. For example, a person sinks their whole existence into a job, a sport, politics, the arts, culture, business or entertainment, and this becomes their faith.

They make this pursuit their whole reason for being and live their lives accordingly. Eventually, for one reason or another, this lets them down in some way and their faith crumbles before them. Finally, they come to the realisation that this cause is false and has not much depth because they have banked their life and soul on its existence. They realise later, when there has been a shift in their understanding, that it only serves a physical purpose. This is the crisis. They then start looking for a more profound meaning to life, so look to the soul within seeking answers.

Quite often this happens with people who place a lot of their life's importance in and around the making of money. They usually lose a great deal of it while trying to hang on to it for the wrong reasons. Their crisis comes when they become broke and have evidence of its transient nature.

The Wall Street crash saw proof of this. Some businessmen committed suicide over paper money, their lives were shattered in an instant. Money is certainly not a good cause or worth dying over. It is what you intend to do with the money that can make it worthwhile obtaining. Another crisis of faith happens when a person's first concept of God is questioned or challenged. Their crisis takes the form of inner questioning about their beliefs of what God is. Who is God? What is divinity? A crisis occurs when their beliefs have been shaken. For most this is a special time and leads to many discoveries. Some look at the history of humankind and of its inherited belief systems, only to realise that there are many other beliefs and so they begin to question their own.

Sometimes an unlearning occurs due to a strict inherited religious dogma brought about through family. When they realise that is in conflict with their own soul's growth, then they have to move on from this mindset. Giving up family religions or not accepting them causes many heartaches, but one cannot deny one's own truth. The rifts will heal eventually.

Another form for many could be that God has never been in their lives, and for whatever reason they decide to seek 'proof' of God's existence in some form or other. These seekers also have a crisis of faith and that is not to have had any belief in God in the first place. This is what happened to me.

Faith

*Faith is a word to describe our beliefs
of self or religion whichever brings relief.
Faith is a belief not based on proof.
To have confidence and trust of a person or truth.
To have faith is to trust in our life's force,
that things will continue on their chartered course.
Whatever happens was meant to be,
so have faith in your life and set yourself free.*

All this really means is that it is painful for any of these people to admit to themselves that their faith, whatever it is, has failed them. Just like the realisation that your parents are fallible and not perfect, so too is the trauma of any crisis of faith.

To journey within is to seek out one's own darkness, mental, physical, emotional and spiritual; to own it, to work with it, and then to balance it back into the light. This is how we give birth to one's true spirit self. Coming back into our conscious awareness of the spirit self is what we are here to do. How you choose to go about this is your own decision. The knowledge that we are truly a divine spark or spirit is a new concept for some. This is who we are and it is who we have lost contact with upon entering this dimension of learning. Part of the work of your soul is to help you come to this understanding.

Our soul leads us down this path of inner knowledge showing us the way so that we may find our spirit. We have need to evolve back into the soul's all-knowing state that brought us here, back to our whole spirit selves in our consciousness. Then, and only then, can we progress along the wheel of rebirth and move onto a new learning realm.

The soul and spirit never die. They are eternal and they literally move on, possibly into other universes or dimensions. Once we are at this stage of spiritual evolvement our journey on earth has taken us full circle.

'Old souls' have been here since the beginning of time and are now helping others to evolve, although there have always been the all-knowing sages around to help evolve the human race. Humankind has been coming out of the darkness and back into the light for a very long time, balancing out the darker sides of our nature with the lighter sides and finding out who we really are in the process.

It is in the acceptance of self realisation that the power of which (the birth, death, and the regeneration of the self,) happens within our own consciousness, that most people have trouble with. This has the added responsibility of our entire being, that of mind, body and spirit. Most people don't want that kind of responsibility. They would prefer to blame everything and everyone in the physical world for their misfortunes rather than take the responsibility of their own choices to participate in their co-created circumstances.

When we search for our soul we seek out knowledge of self. It isn't until we have worked out who we are and why we are the way we are, and how we function, that we come to understand ourselves more fully. Once we have that knowledge and begin to seek ourselves spiritually, we then discover a better reason for existing. It is not merely for survival and comfort, but instead we find true purpose and meaning in our lives.

Soul Connections

Connecting with other souls who are on this level of awareness helps to raise the level of energy felt by everyone. People are connecting for this purpose everywhere. Soul groups are coming back together, some only to share information, some to teach, some to help others evolve spiritually.

They keep in mind their soul's higher purpose which is reflected in their work. These people have evolved faster and, as a result, help evolve others by raising their energy so that they too can come into their own understanding of self and seek their soul's higher purpose.

When we can accept this responsibility then we accept our eternity and rightful place in the universe. We seek our soul's purpose and get on with life, accepting all that is set before us, knowing that there will be challenges for us to fathom and much joy on the journey.

You will know when you have met a highly evolved soul. They remain calm and collected without fear and they know how to enjoy life fully. They have a deeper sense of being and are open and giving. They nurture you when you are with them, giving you a sense of peace and security. You will never leave their presence feeling drained because they don't steal your energy. You will feel uplifted and energised by them.

They will listen to your problems without criticism allowing you to grow at your own pace. You will notice them as always being busy and interesting as they seek all kinds of knowledge which they will be only too willing to share with you should you ask. These people have graduated and have connected with their soul, living in flow with their purpose in life.

Once we can accept that we, meaning our soul and spirit, are eternal and knowing that we return to spirit from whence we came, then it is not necessary for us to fear death. Having got past that hurdle we can get on with living without fear and enjoying the 'now' and look forward to a happy future.

It is the fear of dying that makes us want to control our existence, even after death. We want to preserve our physical body and stay young believing that this will somehow prevent our mortal death. This makeshift control allows the ego to think that it is in charge of our immortality. It is not. It is the soul and ego doing battle again, only this time it is the question of which one is truly eternal.

Many people find emotional comfort in the belief of entering the kingdom of heaven after death, but only if they have obeyed certain religious doctrines and belief. We can create heaven on earth if we want to. We don't have to die to experience it.

We have been trying for some time to sabotage our death, thinking that the mortal physical body was our whole self in total. The deluded ego has been clutching onto this fear of death of the body and so we have sought ways to live longer, to preserve it and make it more perfect. The body has become an idol for false worship.

We use drugs, medicine and surgery to help prove that we are immortal, or at least help us to live longer. When the physical body dies the ego dies with it and so does the mental-emotional body. The soul and its memories of the lessons learned in these experiences are never lost. Ego does not exist within our true spirit or soul. To connect with soul and subjugate your mind and emotions and the body to your spirit's will, is sure death to all ego-born desires. We are not our body, only its keeper.

As we journey within and connect with our soul it helps to bring in our true self. By this I mean we become more honest with ourselves and with others. We develop an unconditional way of giving to others and have, as a result, more integrity with the things we do and say. We learn to let go of any preconceived expectations that we may have of others. Learning all this is true mastery of self, enabling you to use all knowledge of self for your highest good.

Now empowered you can go on into your future, accomplishing whatever you believe your purpose to be during this lifetime. Understanding that you are a soul on a journey through time is hard for some to grasp but this is what you are in essence. You will see those souls that you have connected with this time around in your future lives if need be. So enjoy them now.

Soul Returns

Once our soul returns to the heavens
with knowledge of its journey from this land,
imagine what it will share with the others
about the trek through the ages of man.

Yes, I was there at King Arthur's Round Table
drinking wine with the knights so bold,
and I saw you once again in Egypt
as a scribe for the pharaohs of old.
As their quests in time were unraveled
and many stories began to coincide.
They realised the lessons they had learned
were brought back from the other side.

The soul's growth doesn't stop on this planet
as they ascend it begins anew.
There are no possessions to take when you leave it
accept the wisdom that you have accrued.
So give thanks and enjoy your soul journey
as you wonder and roam this world free.
'Tis a privilege to remain with your friends
whose souls in the future you'll see.

As each soul returns from its journey unknown
with its bounty of invaluable jewels.
It then shares with the others, pearls of wisdom
shedding light on the creator's rules.

In Search of Soul

Chapter 7
Mastery of Self

It was during the pursuit of mastering myself that led to the search for my soul. This journey has taken me full circle now as I remember who I really am. Part of the path of the spiritual warrior's quest is battling with the self, and yet what we all want to become, in reality, we already are.

One day we will remember and awaken from our sleep feeling the presence of our soul; only then will the way home become known to us. Soul searching is becoming consciously aware of who you really are in essence. Learning to express it creatively, while bringing it into being takes courage, trust and wisdom.

> *True mastery is knowingly connecting with your soul through the heart.*

Connecting with your soul will send a vibration through your entire being. This is a love vibration and will be felt by everyone you come in contact with. Your soul is felt through your integrity of purpose, the quality of your physical tuning, and your balance of spirit and mind and heart. Your soul helps you to follow your inner-most passions in life, so that the possibilities you dream of can become your reality.

No longer will you feel self doubt or fear that life is not going to work out for you. This confidence will mean that any challenges placed in your pathway will be met with the knowledge that you can find a solution.

Mastery of self means that you no longer have the need to be validated by everyone else. Even when you or others make mistakes you are able to correct them and forgive yourself or them for any human failings.

Now aligned with the soul your honesty and integrity are reflected within all your dealings with others. This sees you earn respect as a natural part of your evolvement. Family, friends and work colleagues feel more at ease around you, helping communication.

In the search for our soul, we come to an understanding about human nature. We can accept that everyone is at their own levels of growth and awareness with their mind, body and spirit. Realising this helps you stop making harsh judgements and criticisms of others. Instead, you see a much bigger picture, allowing everyone to be who, how and where they need to be at this time; experiencing what they need to experience for growth, just as you do. Knowing that no two people experience the same things in the same way leads to a deeper understanding and acceptance about life.

> *We all see what we want to see,
> feel what we choose to feel,
> and do what we think is right.*

Each person's experience of life is unique, as none of us are the same. We can only share what we learn from our own journey of life in the hope of communicating some pearls of wisdom to others along the way. When we share our truths about life and love with others, we are giving them an opportunity to view it from a different perspective. Sometimes this is all that is needed to open ones eyes to a broader picture. However, do not expect everyone to like what they hear from you. It may challenge and upset their very belief system about themselves.

Sometimes it is better to show them rather than tell them. This allows them to see for themselves what they need to understand. To have mastery of self you need to lead by example, *walking the talk* is how the best teachers teach. If you do not walk your talk then you will become known as a hypocrite.

When you can sit back in silence and witness your true identity you will realise that this is the place of true power. Answers to your questions about life are rarely found in another human. Learn to answer your own questions by connecting with the soul and becoming your own witness.

The Four Steps

Mastering self and allowing more soul to be displayed in our life involves four main steps.

The first step is to **know** the self. There can be no mastery of self without knowledge from the higher self passed onto the lower self first. When we can accept and work with this knowledge about the self we are becoming truly enlightened.

The second step is to *love* the self. We cannot expect others to love us unless we learn to love ourselves first. Opening your heart to accepting the self is a giant step to self love. True love will come your way upon accepting love from the self.

The third step is to *heal* the self. By this I mean that we need to look at all aspects of the self and take the responsibility to heal those parts of us that are not whole yet, whether they be of mind, body or spirit, bringing your self into more balance.

It is because of this need for self healing that we've seen the rise in the development of new energetic self-healing modalities. Things like massage, aromatherapy, reflexology, meditation, reiki, rolfing, pulsing, cranial-sacral and the like are now being excepted as necessary in our society, helping to heal the spirit by releasing negativity trapped in our systems.

I became a Reiki Master during the pursuit of health, well-being and spiritual growth. Reiki is a hands-on healing modality that uses life-force energy, which help cure my mothers cronic fatigue.

The fourth and final step is to *share* what you learn and know with others. This is how you put back into society.

Every time you share your wisdom to those who ask, you are helping to lift the whole vibration of humankind. The more we help each other and shed light on those aspects of self that have been hidden away, with truth and love, the more we will grow as a people.

When all four aspects have been put into place then you are truly the master of self. Now, with the help of Reiki, I wish to share my gathered knowledge with those whom I meet. This has not always been easy for me to do. However, the more I share and teach others with truth and love the more acceptance and freedom I receive.

Trust and Transformation

Harnessing the workings of your mind leads to transformation. As you take control of how you think and feel, you are choosing to create the future with your will and intention, aligned with the soul's purpose. Seeking the strength and wisdom, through your ability to love, helps bring this transformation into action. It is displayed in your life through the deeds you undertake and the words that you speak. By mastering the self you are able to manifest your secret dreams through the process of transformation.

Loving the self means trusting the self. Without trust, there is no love. Trust in the power of love and see the transformation that you can bring about in your life. Trust is opening yourself up with love, not understanding. You cannot love the self or others with the mind; you must listen with the heart. This is the way of the soul and true mastery.

> Don't learn everything with the mind.
> Intellect can be an empty vessel
> without love to sail it.

Every time you are possessed by an emotion that you cannot control, know that it does not belong to you. Trust the process of releasing your fears and negative emotions with love. By filling the emotion with the power of love and releasing it to the universe, it is transformed. It is just like muddy water running into the sea, becoming clearer with every wave. Seek help and facilitation if need be.

Learn to let go of these destructive powers, which would inhibit your growth. Instead, allow your soul to experience mystery and magic. When living the ordinary life in an extraordinary way it becomes magical. Magic is part of mastery and what we are all looking to experience in our lives. But the minute you try to hold onto it, to claim it, you lose it.

Out of the mysteries of creation comes the magic of life. When you live your life out of the passion for existence, you will find true magic exists.

Learning to Nurture and Balance

Harmony can only be found when you begin to find the balance between the physical and spiritual aspects of your life. Imagine yourself in the centre of your body. To the north is your emotional self, to the south is your mental self, to the west is your physical self and to the east is your spiritual self. As you stand in the centre are they in balance and in harmony?

Ask yourself, do you spend as much time in the emotional (north) as you do in the mental (south)? Are they balanced? Reflect on whether you spend more time in your physical (west) than you do in the spiritual (east).

To function properly there must be harmony and balance within all these aspects of self.

Listen to your soul and bring yourself back into balance by adjusting you actions or behaviour patterns in all directions. This is the mark of true mastery.

> *For there to be true harmony there must be balance.*

It can be achieved simply, by taking care of your body with diet and exercise. It brings a greater awareness to any exchanges you do with money. Protecting, nourishing and loving your family, while expressing your integrity through helping society come into balance also. Your spirit is made available to the knowledge along the path to higher consciousness. All helping to bring you into balance.

This kind of balance sees you prepared in your physical life for higher spiritual learning. With true balance in your life, it is easier to listen and feel the needs of your soul. Learn to take time out, nurture your soul, and heal any wounds that may occur from time to time. Life is about give and take and that includes the self.

Listen to all aspects of your being and when something feels out of balance take time out to do some healing in that area.

Learn to see past any social barriers, which cloud the visions of men and women alike and nurture the soul. This is an act of mastery, knowing when to retreat and do without doing.

When you nurture the soul, you find the sacred places of hidden dreams deep in your heart. There maybe times when your vision of these dreams becomes distorted. Everything will look gloomy or cloudy. This is a test of will and growth because it is time for the all-knowing soul to be illuminated. You will begin to see the sacredness of life within every object. You will develop true vision and your spirituality becomes much stronger, helping you to see past the illusions of fear and disharmony.

As you let go and relax into the flow of life, secure with all aspects of yourself, you will be filled with a sense of calm and peace. This is the gift of the soul that can never leave you once it is known. You begin to bloom when you move with the flow of your eternal soul's life.

Searching for soul is the search for wholeness, love and fulfillment with purpose. Those of you who embark on this conscious search will not fail.

Your soul is calling from the depths of your being for you to begin to master your life.

S'Roya Rose TAROT
78 Card Deck and Guidebook

Modern Goddess Oracle
60 Cards & Guidebook

Blue Moon Oracle
52 Cards & Guidebook

The Art of Meaningful Living
Simple wisdom for the 21st century.

CHAKRAS
& Their Hidden Wisdom

The Third EYE
Psychic Secrets for aspiring Mystics

Embracing the Power
of the Goddess

TAROT A Sacred Doorway
A must have Tarot Compendium
for the Modern Cosmic Sage!

REIKI A Transformational
Spiritual Healing Pathway

For more information on,
or to stock or purchase any of
S'Roya's book titles or oracle
card decks or magazines,
please visit her website:
www.sroyarose.com
or alternatively
www.phoenixdistribution.com.au

3RD EYE
PUBLICATIONS

About the Author
S'Roya Rose:

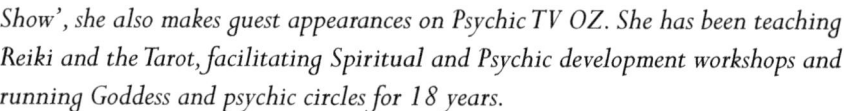

S'Roya is a gifted clairvoyant Psycho Therapist, and well known Australian Celebrity Psychic Medium, she is an initiating High Priestess of the Goddess, who works with the angelic, elemental, Ascended Masters, ancient Mystics, the Animal clans, and other cosmic Shamanic realms, able to connect with spirit guides and deceased loved ones.

Having appeared nationally on channel Seven's 'New Age of Aquarius' show, and on channel nine's 'Sunday Show', she also makes guest appearances on Psychic TV OZ. She has been teaching Reiki and the Tarot, facilitating Spiritual and Psychic development workshops and running Goddess and psychic circles for 18 years.

An accomplished writer, she's has been active in shifting consciousness publishing various book titles having been the creatrix and editor of many spiritual magazines ie; DejaVu, Dharma, BlackRose, Goddess Guru & Avalon. Recently she launched her amazing Tarot, and Modern Goddess Oracle deck and her latest fabulous Blue Moon Oracle wisdom cards.

A natural born Mystic of the modern age she is respected as being a wise goddess, her counsel being constantly sought after, usually bookings must be made weeks in advance. To book a personal session, via Skype or Phone Reading with S'Roya or a Healing Psycho Therapy session, simply email her on: email@sroyarose.com

S'Roya is a practicing Initiating Priestess of the Goddess, a Reiki Master Teacher, Psychic Therapist and Empowerment Specialist. She teaches advanced Metaphysics in seminars and workshops; also holding regular Circles, yearly Goddess Retreats.
She is available for individual face to face consultations, offering Mentoring and group Coaching and Life Readings via skype and phone.

Website: www.sroyarose.com
Facebook: http://www.facebook.com/SRoyaRose

www.ingramcontent.com/pod-product-compliance
Ingram Content Group UK Ltd.
Pitfield, Milton Keynes, MK11 3LW, UK
UKHW022212230426
12048UKWH00016BA/805